C. S. Lewis

Twayne's English Authors Series

Kinley E. Roby, Editor

Northeastern University

TEAS 442

C. S. LEWIS
(1898–1963)
Photograph by Wolf Suschitzky
Courtesy of The Marion E. Wade Collection,
Wheaton College, Wheaton, Illinois

C. S. Lewis

By Joe R. Christopher

Tarleton State University

Twayne Publishers
A Division of G.K. Hall & Co. • Boston

C. S. Lewis

Joe R. Christopher

Copyright © 1987 by G.K. Hall & Co.
All Rights Reserved
Published by Twayne Publishers
A Division of G.K. Hall & Co.
70 Lincoln Street
Boston, Massachusetts 02111

Copyediting supervised by Lewis DeSimone
Book production by Marne Sultz
Book design by Barbara Anderson

Typeset in 11 pt. Garamond
by Modern Graphics, Inc., Weymouth, Massachusetts

Printed on permanent/durable acid-free paper
and bound in the United States of America

Library of Congress Cataloging in Publication Data

Christopher, Joe R.
  C. S. Lewis.

  (Twayne's English authors series ; TEAS 442)
  Bibliography: p. 136
  Includes index.
  1. Lewis, C. S. (Clive Staples), 1898–1963—Criticism and
interpretation. I. Title. II. Series.
PR6023.E926Z64   1987   828'.91209   86–25757
ISBN 0–8057–6944–7

For Paul G. Ruggiers,
who first guided me through Dante's three realms

Contents

About the Author

Joe R. Christopher, Associate Professor of English at Tarleton State University, was the cocompiler of *C. S. Lewis: Writings about Him and His Works* (1974). He has published some fifty articles and bibliographies in whole or part on C. S. Lewis. He has also published articles on such diverse writers as the Pearl Poet, Coleridge, Edgar Allan Poe, Mark Twain, Tennyson, Dorothy L. Sayers, Ellery Queen, and J. R. R. Tolkien. Dr. Christopher has chaired sessions of Contemporary Literature, Anglo-Irish Literature (twice), and Christianity and Literature at South Central Modern Language Association meetings. Besides papers given at SCMLA, he has read scholarly studies at meetings of the Modern Language Association, the Conference on Christianity and Literature (both Southwest and Southcentral Divisions), and the Mythopoeic Society. Outside of his professional area, he has published over fifty poems and half a dozen short stories in journals and magazines, and a drama by him has received an academic production.

Preface

C. S. Lewis is an interesting example of an author who, while not usually considered a "man of letters," wrote in a number of different kinds. His popular reputation comes from his Christian books—apologetics, *The Screwtape Letters,* such Christian-flavored fiction as the children's books about Narnia. His scholarly repute is based on studies of medieval and Renaissance literature. And, as the chapter titles to this study indicate, he also wrote autobiography and philosophy.

Literary fluidity is not the same thing as greatness, or any hack writer would be up with Shakespeare. But the number of books in the secondary bibliography indicates, in Lewis's case, a continuing interest in his ideas and expressions. The use of *expressions* is important: Lewis is, at his best—preeminently in *Till We Have Faces*—the equal of the major authors of his period. (Fuller claims appear in the tenth chapter.) It is also true that Lewis's books in general, while almost always well written in comparison with others in their genres, often have fascinating flaws in them.

The approach in this book is in terms of Lewis himself and his artistry. Lewis disliked the first of these emphases, calling it (in the title of one of his volumes) the personal heresy. In this, Lewis was typical of one side of his period, since T. S. Eliot also denied that the artist was the concern of criticism. Probably they were both, in part, reacting against the excessive bio-criticism (and idolatry) of the nineteenth century, as well as the Freudianism of the twentieth. Obviously, in some sense, they were right. The art matters, not the artist. But I do not attempt pure criticism here, and I find it interesting to note passages of biographical interest in the various works. Major references by Lewis to other members of the Inklings, the Oxford literary circle of 1938 to 1949, are part of this biographical concern. Also, though not so directly, are references to Dante, for the Italian poet was a major influence.

Except for this biographical emphasis, I have tried to approach Lewis's writings strictly as literature. For example, in the discussion of Lewis's *Miracles* I fault the revised chapter for being more abstract; a philosopher or theologian probably would praise its gain in precision. This approach has led to some comparisons with other literature in Lewis's various genres and also to a tendency to not ignore, but certainly not greatly stress, Lewis's Christian beliefs. Behind the latter is my assumption that literature qua literature proves itself by a meaning that can be read universally, after due allowance is made for its particular origin. (Sometimes, however, I have been satisfied merely to suggest how Lewis may be approached as an interesting example of a period author; not all of his works are universal in my sense.)

Of course, the sophisticated reader always approaches a work from a different "persuasion" with a willing suspension of disbelief; but for the work to be vital for him or her, to be more than merely appreciated and enjoyed, to affect the reader's sensibilities, reason, or imagination, it has to speak beyond its cultural or other limits. This is an ancient paradox in the reading of literature: a delight in the details of a particular time and place, even if invented, or in an expression of a particular sensibility (even in a particular dialectic, as in Lewis), combined with a desire for some type of nonparticular, nonparochial, applicability. Gimpel, in Isaac Bashevis Singer's "Gimpel the Fool," is not just a figure of (imaginative) Jewish history in Poland. The naif (holy or not) always has problems with society.

Matters of artistry include, always, structural analyses of the full-length books. (Because of the number of Lewis's volumes, it is only book-length, prose works that are of concern here—although some essays and poems are mentioned in passing.) Other artistic matters vary according to the genre of the works: rhetorical strategy in the nonfiction, for example.

The organization of this book, except for the two framing chapters on Lewis's life and the significance of his writings, is roughly chronological. The chapter on autobiographies comes first because *The Pilgrim's Regress* appeared in 1933, the first of his books of prose. The later autobiographies are discussed in this chapter in chronological order, and the other chapters have the same sort of generic sorting. This allows the reader of the whole book to see Lewis beginning in prose with a spiritual autobiography after his conversion to Christianity, and developing into the scholarly and religious writer who achieved his reputations. There is some arbitrariness as to placement of the chapters. For example, the chapter on moral philosophy is set before the apologetics because it prepares for the religious writing that follows, and because Lewis's philosophical training preceded his return to Christianity. The chapters on the prose romances are placed last for rhetorical emphasis: fiction is more likely than nonfiction to be significant art, and it tends to outlast nonfiction in the affections of generations of readers. Thus, it is appropriate to end with what are probably Lewis's most enduring works.

Acknowledgments are due to various persons: to James Como and Kathryn Lindskoog, who looked at an outline of this book years ago and made some suggestions; to Rose Ann Kincannon, Nancy Bond, Ruth Winfrey, Patti Wright, and Mary Etzel, who typed drafts of parts of this book; to Lynn Christopher, who got increasingly irritated as I took longer and longer to get finished; to the Tarleton State University Research Committee, which twice gave me summer grants to work on this project; to P. Allen Hargis and Marjorie Lamp Mead of the Wade Collection, who gave some last-minute help; to Sylvia E. Bowman, Kinley Roby, and various editors at Twayne who put up with false starts, extensive revisions, and great slowness; and to Athenaide Dallett, also at Twayne, who directed the final steps of the writing.

Joe R. Christopher

Tarleton State University

ABOUT THE AUTHOR

Joe R. Christopher is associate professor of English at Tarleton State University, Texas. He is the co-author of *C. S. Lewis: An Annotated Checklist of Writings about Him and His Works* and has contributed to *The Longing for a Form: Essays on the Fiction of C. S. Lewis*. His published works include numerous articles on C. S. Lewis and J. R. R. Tolkien.

Chronology

1898   29 November, Clive Staples Lewis born in Belfast, Ireland, to Albert James Lewis, solicitor, and Florence Augusta (Hamilton).

1905   Family moves to the edge of town, where Lewis writes his juvenilia about Animal-land.

1905–1908   Experiences *Sehnsucht*.

1908   Death of his mother from cancer. Sent to Wynard School, Hertfordshire.

1910   Briefly attends Campbell College, Belfast.

1911   Sent to Cherbourg School, Malvern, Worchestershire; loses his Christian faith while there. Moved by Norse myths; return of *Sehnsucht*.

1913   Sent to Malvern College.

1914   Friendship with Arthur Greeves. Begins with a private tutor, W. T. Kirkpatrick, in Great Bookham, Surrey.

1916   Reads George MacDonald's *Phantastes*.

1917   April, takes up residency at University College, Oxford. June, joins a cadet battalion of the University Officers' Training Corps. November, goes to France as an officer.

1918   Wounded during the Battle of Arras. After the war, "adopts" Janie Moore as a foster mother.

1919   *Spirits in Bondage,* as by Clive Hamilton. Returns to Oxford; meets Owen Barfield soon after.

1922   Receives a Bachelor of Arts degree.

1924   Begins a one-year appointment in philosophy at University College, Oxford.

1925   Begins as a tutor in English, Magdalen College, Oxford.

1926   *Dymer,* as by Clive Hamilton. Meets J. R. R. Tolkien.

1928   Death of father from cancer.

1929   Converts on philosophical grounds from atheism to theism.

1930   Purchases "The Kilns," a home on the outskirts of Oxford. "The Nameless Isle" faircopied.

1931   Talk with Hugo Dyson and Tolkien on Christianity as myth come true. Accepts Christ while riding in the sidecar of his brother's motorcycle on the way to Whipsnade Zoo.

1933   *The Pilgrim's Regress.*

1936   *The Allegory of Love.*

1937   The Inklings begin meeting about this time.

1938   *Out of the Silent Planet* (first of the Ransom Trilogy).

1939   *Rehabilitations and Other Essays. The Personal Heresy,* with E. M. W. Tillyard. Charles Williams moves to Oxford.

1940   *The Problem of Pain.*

1941   Begins giving religious talks at military bases. Gives radio addresses on "Right and Wrong: A Clue to the Meaning of the Universe?" (published as part of *Broadcast Talks,* 1942)—the first of four series of war-time radio talks.

1942   *The Screwtape Letters. A Preface to "Paradise Lost."* The Socratic Club founded at Oxford; Lewis is president until 1954.

1943   *Christian Behaviour* (radio talks). *Perelandra* (second of the Ransom Trilogy).

1944   *The Abolition of Man. Beyond Personality* (radio talks).

1945   *That Hideous Strength* (third of the Ransom Trilogy). *The Great Divorce.* Williams dies.

1946   *George Macdonald: An Anthology* (edited).

1947   *Miracles. Essays Presented to Charles Williams* (edited).

1948   *Arthurian Torso,* including material by Williams.

1949   *"Transposition" and Other Addresses.* Last meeting of the Inklings.

1950 *The Lion, the Witch and the Wardrobe* (Narnian series).

1951 *Prince Caspian* (Narnian series). Janie Moore dies.

1952 *Mere Christianity* (containing the three books of radio talks). *The Voyage of the "Dawn Treader"* (Narnian series). Meets Helen Joy Davidman Gresham.

1953 *The Silver Chair* (Narnian series).

1954 *The Horse and His Boy* (Narnian series). *English Literature in the Sixteenth Century, Excluding Drama.* Gives inaugural lecture as Professor of Medieval and Renaissance Literature at Cambridge University.

1955 *The Magician's Nephew* (Narnian series). *Surprised by Joy.*

1956 *The Last Battle* (Narnian series). *Till We Have Faces.* Marries Joy Davidman at the Oxford registry office.

1957 Religious marriage to Joy Davidman.

1958 *Reflections on the Psalms.* Appointed to the Archbishops' Commission to Revise the Psalter (with six others), producing *The Revised Psalter* (1966). "The Four Loves" recorded for American radio.

1960 *The Four Loves. Studies in Words. "The World's Last Night" and Other Essays.* April, trip to Greece with Joy Davidman. July, death of Joy Davidman from cancer.

1961 *A Grief Observed,* as by N. W. Clerk. *An Experiment in Criticism.*

1962 *They Asked for a Paper.*

1963 22 November, dies. Soon after, appears twice to J. B. Phillips, the New Testament translator (according to Phillips).

1964 *Letters to Malcolm: Chiefly on Prayer. The Discarded Image.* (The last two books prepared by Lewis for the press.)

Chapter One
A Romantic and Argumentative Life
Childhood (1898–1911)

Clive Staples Lewis—"Jack" to relatives and friends since his child-hood—was an Ulsterman by birth, born in Belfast in 1898, before the partition of Ireland in 1921. Although Lewis occasionally refers to himself as an Irishman and with fair regularity returned to Ireland on vacations, his writings are little influenced by his birthplace, with the exception of his autobiography and some lyrics—mostly involving Irish myth—in his first published book, *Spirits in Bondage* (1919). The discussions of Irish politics that he heard at home while growing up seem to have wearied him of such topics; in later years he refused to read newspapers. Further, he served in the British army in World War I, something that he as an Irish national did not have to do.[1]

One influence of Lewis's region is important: from his nursery windows, he saw the Castlereagh Hills. He says in *Surprised by Joy* that they taught him longing, the type of romantic longing that is called *Sehnsucht*.[2] In *Bright Shadow of Reality*, Corbin Scott Carnell finds four recurring images in Lewis's writings to convey the concept of *Sehnsucht*: distant hills, an exotic garden, an island (often in the far east or the far west), and sweet music; the plots Lewis uses with these are usually quests, sometimes involving faerieland.[3] Some of the lyrics in the last section of *Spirits in Bondage* describe these quests from his then non-Christian perspective. Lewis's fullest *theological* discussion of this experience is in one of his sermons, "The Weight of Glory" (1941).[4]

The other side of Lewis's personality—the nonromantic—is his argumentative and rationalistic aspects. John Wain has written, "Lewis's father was a lawyer, and the first thing that strikes one upon opening any of Lewis's books is that he is always persuading, always arguing a case."[5] This tendency was reinforced by Lewis's

1

private schooling under W. T. Kirkpatrick, who continually asked Lewis to define his terms and defend his assumptions. In later years, besides using Kirkpatrick's methods on the students he was tutoring, Lewis met his peers with arguments—for example, defeating E. M. W. Tillyard in a debate over the topics they had argued in the essays of *The Personal Heresy* and losing to G. E. M. Anscombe at a meeting of the Oxford Socratic Club when she challenged one of his arguments in *Miracles*.[6]

Other aspects of the later Lewis can be attributed (with the usual reservations that any arguments of this sort have to make) to Lewis's youth. Perhaps the early death of his mother—when he was nine— and his subsequent emotional estrangement from his father contributed to his tendency toward objectivity and avoidance of the personal. On the other hand, Lewis has said that the personality differences between his parents caused his self-containment (SJ, chap. 1). Whatever the cause, Nevill Coghill's comment is to the point, speaking of Lewis in his days as a student at Oxford: "He differed in his youth from most others of his age by seeming to have no sexual problems or preoccupations, or need to talk about them if he had them: and it was with surprise that I read of the 'brown girls' in his first prose work, *The Pilgrim's Regress*."[7] (The *seeming* is the point; more will be said below.) A number of critics have noted a great impersonality in many of Lewis's writings.

Another possible influence of his mother's death and his paternal estrangement is Lewis's "adoption" of Janie Moore as a foster mother after World War I (her son, Paddy Moore, one of Lewis's wartime companions, had been killed in combat). Since Mrs. Moore appears to have been (at her worst) irrational, quarrelsome, and antireligious, Lewis's depiction of the "patient's" mother in *The Screwtape Letters*, and like figures elsewhere, may have been indebted to her.

Perhaps Lewis's childhood period of imaginative play (Animal-Land) that was shared by his brother (India) prepared him to be an author who was ready to borrow from his friends. For an obvious example, in *That Hideous Strength* he has Merlin refer to Tolkien's Númenor (as "Numinor"). Owen Barfield and Charles Williams were influential on Lewis's ideas, and this question of borrowings is a large one in Lewis studies. Humphrey Carpenter, in *The Inklings*, complains that Lewis's poems are mostly imitations of earlier styles (pp. 31, 244). Certainly, as will become clear later in this book,

Lewis again and again borrows from Dante's *Divine Comedy*. (George Sayer has called Dante Lewis's "favourite poet.")[8]

Lewis, in his essay "Christianity and Literature" (1939), says that modern critical theory praises originality and related concepts, while the New Testament tells the Christian he is to imitate Christ. Thus Lewis surmises that the Christian author will not strive to be "creative" or "original," but will attempt to capture already given great truths in his writings (when writing serious works). Lewis goes further, to suggest the Christian will write, if he can, in established genres (presumably to avoid originality). Thus, whether or not a reader likes what Lewis is doing in his fiction and (to some degree) nonfiction, he is working on a consistent aesthetic basis. This is not to argue that Lewis did not end up with originality.

These literary and other influences from his childhood—*Sehnsucht*, argumentativeness, a tendency toward literary borrowings from friends, a personal insecurity from the death of his mother—can be taken as the inward aspects of that period. Outwardly, Lewis grew up in a well-read, well-to-do household in Belfast, and was sent away to various "public schools," mostly in England, as was typical of his class. The first school was a disaster, the headmaster evidently being mad (he was institutionalized after the collapse of the school). During his time at the third, Lewis lost his Christian belief; at the fourth, he reacted against the whole public-school ethos. But, as *Surprised by Joy* makes clear, Lewis's life was in two parts: the outward, day-to-day life—Irish relatives, academic successes and failures—was of less importance than the imaginative inward life— the latter mostly involving delight in, and call of, *Sehnsucht* through nature and Norse myth.

Adolescence and Early Adulthood (1911–1932)

Lewis's following years show the same split. Outwardly, Lewis went to the private tutor mentioned before, studying mainly the classics and absorbing rationalism. He took his entrance examination at Oxford University and was awarded a scholarship at University College. (He never passed the mathematical requirements but continued after World War I under a dispensation for soldiers.) Soon after the war and the adoption of the foster mother and her daughter, Lewis met Owen Barfield at Oxford, who became a life-long friend (and sometimes philosophical opponent)—as described in *Surprised by Joy* (chap. 13)—and later a member of the Inklings.

Lewis's Oxford career was successful: a first in Honour Moderations (Greek and Latin), after about a year and a half; a first in Greats (philosophy and ancient history), for his Bachelor of Arts; and a first in English Language and Literature, a year later, for a second teaching field. He received a one-year appointment in philosophy at University College, and then became a tutor in English at Magdalen College. This remained his profession until 1954. In 1926, at a faculty meeting, Lewis met J. R. R. Tolkien, who became one of his closest friends until the 1950s.

In these early years Lewis was trying to be a poet. After *Spirits in Bondage,* he published *Dymer* (1926), the story of a young man's rebellion against society and his seeking of the Spirit behind *Sehnsucht.* He completed two other, more successful narrative poems: "The Nameless Isle" (1930), a rehandling of motifs from Mozart's *Magic Flute* (1791), and "The Queen of Drum" (finished ca. 1933–34), in which the Queen rejects the Christian faith for faerie. *Faerie* in this poem stands for *Sehnsucht,* and obviously Lewis did not yet see that longing as leading to God; but in *The Pilgrim's Regress* (1933), of the same period, the Christian end for his romantic desires became clear—and remained Lewis's formulation for the rest of his life.

Other aspects of Lewis's sensibilities are important. One probably developed after puberty, although the evidence does not appear until he and Arthur Greeves, his closest Irish friend, discussed their emotional sexual desires, walking up and down a road one night, evidently during the Christmas season of 1916–17, when Lewis was eighteen.[9] Greeves was a homosexual; Lewis, a heterosexual sadist. No doubt Lewis used that aspect of his temperament, slightly modified, when he developed Fairy Hardcastle in *That Hideous Strength.*

An interesting account appears in Lewis's letters to Greeves, collected as *They Stand Together.* While Lewis was at Oxford in June of 1917, before he served in World War I, he got drunk at a party, verbally revealed his sexual bias, and had a suggestion made that he should read de Sade (pp. 188, 191). He does not say he did read him, but given Lewis's tendency to read almost everything—as revealed in these letters—it would be surprising if he did not. At any rate, thereafter almost all references to his own sexual attitudes disappear. Lewis probably looked at de Sade and reacted strongly in the opposite direction. By the time he had gone through the war, a year after the drinking episode, he was saying that a Spirit exists and that beauty is its call to man (p. 217); matter, physical nature, and the body are evil (pp. 214, 218). In short, Lewis was starting in the direction of religious faith. This causal reading may not be correct; but even if it is, it does not invalidate Lewis's later Christian position: Christianity assumes that all persons are sinners and that only by means of grace can their sins be overcome. Further, Lewis's anti-body attitude explains why he did not discuss his sexuality with Nevill Coghill during their undergraduate years: he did not discuss what he was rejecting (and probably attempting to repress).

Some of the most important biographical events were for Lewis philosophic and religious. He was raised in the Church of Ireland— that is, the Anglican Church—and seems to have tried to practice his faith, particularly through prayers, in his early years. He lost his faith about his thirteenth year, partially due to the usual upsets about the time of puberty, to learning about the occult and realizing the pagan gods were taken seriously by the original authors, and to a pessimism based ultimately on a feeling of lack of design in the universe. A number of Lewis's lyrics in *Spirits in Bondage* reflect this period, as well as some reflecting the subsequent period of dualism (Spirit/beauty vs. physicality/evil). In 1929 Lewis argued himself into a belief in theism, and two years later he accepted Jesus as God's Son. The first step was entirely philosophical. Although the second involved J. R. R. Tolkien and Hugo Dyson convincing him that Christianity could be accepted as myth-come-true—that the best pagan myths became fact in Christ—this acceptance of Jesus as divine was much more a personal encounter with God. The first two autobiographies are based on this pattern of going toward atheism and then returning to Christianity; *Till We Have Faces,* among the fiction, shows the same design. Tied to Lewis's return was his reading in 1916 of George MacDonald's *Phantastes* (1858), which Lewis later declared baptized his imagination before he was able to work out his intellectual problems; thus MacDonald shows up as Lewis's spiritual guide in his other-world fantasy, *The Great Divorce.*

Lewis's *Surprised by Joy* is surprisingly reticent on the surface details of his Christian conversion. The discussion with Tolkien and Dyson is reduced to one generalized sentence (chap. 14). The time of Lewis's final acceptance of Christ—while riding in the sidecar of his brother's motorcycle on the way to Whipsnade Zoo—is stripped of his brother and the motorcycle (chap. 15). But the last three chapters of that book are more internalized than the first twelve.

Owen Barfield has suggested that faith reinforced Lewis's objectivity that he had brought from childhood—if not something more. Barfield describes how Lewis seemed to deliberately suppress self-knowledge of any sort beyond awareness of his own sins. "Anything beyond that he sharply suspected, both in himself and others, as a symptom of spiritual megalomania. At best, there was so much else, in letters and in life, that he found much *more* interesting."[10]

Adulthood (1932–1963)

Lewis's later years are spent in tutoring, lecturing, and writing, for the most part, not in radical changes. In the 1930s, his brother and he went on annual walking tours during academic vacations. (Their third tour, 1–6 January 1934, is described in the printed selections of W. H. Lewis's diaries, *Brothers and Friends* [1982].) The Inklings—Tolkien, Lewis, occasionally Barfield, at periods Dyson, and others—began to meet weekly in the 1930s during university terms, usually on Thursday nights, usually in Lewis's Magdalen rooms; Charles Williams joined when Oxford University Press was moved to Oxford in 1939. The World War II years were the major ones for this group of writers to meet and read their works in progress to each other: Lewis's lyrics, fiction, and apologetics; Tolkien's *Lord of the Rings*; Williams's Arthurian poems and last novel. On 20 October 1949 was the last meeting.

The 1950s broke some patterns. Lewis's foster mother died in 1951; in 1954 Lewis gave up Oxford for Cambridge, becoming a professor there—which meant no more tutoring; in 1956 Lewis married Joy Davidman, an American author and divorcée, who died in 1960 from cancer. Lewis himself, suffering a variety of ailments, died in 1963.

On Lewis's adult learning there is little need to dilate. Almost every writer on Lewis speaks of his wide reading in literature—classical, medieval, and British, especially—and his retentive memory. He had his limits—a tendency to quote from memory, which often made minor changes; inaccuracy in minor copy work; and a propensity to see life in the periods he studied through the literature, rather than vice versa. He wrote in a letter to Derek Brewer, "Haven't you discovered yet that I'm not a Scholar but only a Learned Man?"[11] Of the actual content of his writings in scholarly fields more will be said in later chapters; but Derek Brewer's comment that he was a romance critic, not a tragedy critic, is a good general guide.[12]

Related to his scholarship, Kathleen Raine noted, was "a kind of boyish greatness" that caused learning to be for him "a joyful and inexhaustible game."[13] Humphrey Carpenter, however, has taken the term *boyishness* as one of the key terms of Lewis's personality, pointing to his tendency to reread children's books, to use schoolboy slang to express enthusiasm for books (particularly in his letters), and to such slapstick scenes as Weston and Devine at the council meeting near the end of *Out of the Silent Planet,* in which Weston treats the Martians as primitive natives and gets his head dunked in water (Carpenter, 218–20). This is a charge hard to refute, although it might be pointed out that Shakespeare also wrote some slapstick scenes. Certainly, Lewis's "boyishness" does not mean a lack of knowledge of the adult world, although this knowledge is expressed in largely moral terms in Lewis's nonfiction.

Finally, his marriage. The details around his nuptials with (Helen) Joy Davidman (Gresham) are complicated, since Lewis went through two marriage ceremonies with her, a year apart—the first a civil marriage, out of friendship, he told friends, and the second a religious ceremony, out of love. But so far as his writings are concerned, the influences are less complicated: the use of aspects of her personality and appearance in his heroine of *Till We Have Faces,* a loss of the male chauvinism that characterized some of his earlier writings, a knowledgeable treatment of eros in *The Four Loves,* and his reaction to her death in *A Grief Observed.* There are also three references to her death ("the great blow") in *Letters to Malcolm* (Letters 4, 8, 22) and three sonnets written to her—"Joys That Sting," "Old Poets Remembered," and "As the Ruin Falls" (in *Poems*). The second of these lyrics indicates that Lewis felt in his marriage the sort of passion that courtly love celebrates, and the third suggests that his wife was breaking down the self-containment mentioned above. Lewis also wrote a poem for her ashes' depository.[14]

This sketch of Lewis's life inevitably has suggested that the two terms of romantic and rationalist are not enough to contain the man.

True. But in Lewis's best-known works, he is most often being mythic or argumentative. The terms do not contain him, but they point to a useful, and legitimate, way of first approaching his writings.

Chapter Two
The Autobiographer

Why did C. S. Lewis write any autobiographies? In *The Personal Heresy*, he argues that the modern tendency to try to make contact with an author through his works is in error. Surely, autobiographies are the closest sort of intellectual contact, and they also give evidence of what was important to the author for application to his other works.

On the other hand, Lewis knew the religious tradition of autobiographies, such as St. Augustine's *Confessions* and John Bunyan's *Grace Abounding to the Chief of Sinners,* as an aid to later Christians. His first two autobiographies, the allegorical *Pilgrim's Regress* and the history of his early life, *Surprised by Joy,* are in this tradition. *A Grief Observed,* which tells of his struggle for faith after his wife's death, belongs in the same tradition, although there are not so many treatments of the struggle to retain faith, as of the first coming to it—or, in the case of Lewis's first two, the coming back to it.

Still, there must be something more to Lewis's impulse. After his philosophic conversion to theism, but before his return to Christianity, he wrote a seventy-two page account of how he had reached a belief in God. This work, not yet published, shows that there was a continuing desire to explain himself, despite "the personal heresy."

The books in this chapter are certainly diverse. *The Pilgrim's Regress* is intellectualized in its form, perhaps the only way Lewis could describe his life in those days. *Surprised by Joy* and *A Grief Observed* are more typical of the introverted autobiography, although the former includes more external material than the latter. *Surprised by Joy* also prepared the way for Lewis's *Till We Have Faces*: until he had looked inside himself in a narrative, he did not look deeply into a fictional character.

Although they are certainly autobiographical in one sense or another, the four books of Lewis's letters so far collected have been omitted from this discussion despite there being a long tradition of reading letters for literary merits. The most important for understanding Lewis's teen years is his correspondence with Arthur Greeves, *They Stand Together*.

The Pilgrim's Regress (1933, 1943)

In 1933, when Lewis wrote his first account of his Christian conversion, he was already working on *The Allegory of Love,* having started on the first chapter in 1928. The scholarly work could not have been the direct influence on *The Pilgrim's Regress* since the love traditions are not those used here. But knowledge and love of allegory are basic to both books.

It would be easy to assume *The Pilgrim's Regress* is indebted to John Bunyan's *The Pilgrim's Progress,* particularly in light of Lewis's subtitle in manuscript: *Pseudo-Bunyan's Periplus*. But the only correspondences are very general ones: both involve allegorical quests toward Heaven by foot journey. Probably the work most like Lewis's in the history of English literature is not Bunyan's book but William Langland's fourteenth-century poem, *Piers Plowman*. Langland has the same mixture, if not quite in the same proportions, of social satire, intellectual discussion, and religious vision. (This is not an argument of influence; the similarity is one of human experience.)

This mixture and its resulting tone is not typical of Lewis's works, although *The Great Divorce* is something like it (with a lighter proportion of intellectual discussion). The published subtitle of *The Pilgrim's Regress* indicates the approach: *An Allegorical Apology for Christianity, Reason, and Romanticism. Apology (apologia)* means "defense": Lewis defends his positions both by satire of others' views and a philosophical discussion of his view.

But first the autobiographical aspects of the book should be considered. The pilgrim of *The Pilgrim's Regress* is John, whose story begins about the time he is able to walk; he is a child, living in Puritania. (Lewis objected when a publisher suggested that Puritania = Ulster, but it is probable that they lie in the same geographic area, Puritania being simply wider in its scope and including a number of late Victorian areas; since the days of Lewis's childhood, it may be said to have shrunk in size.) Some of John's adventures as he grows up may not be Lewis's, but simply occurrences typical of the period. For example, in the first chapter, John visits a Steward (clergyman) who talks with him very pleasantly except when he clasps on a mask of an elderly gentleman and tells John of the rules he must obey. Somewhat later, in the city Eschropolis (Scab Town—built of steel), John hears some poetry recited by two of the Clevers. One is Victoriana—a woman of about fifty, dressed in exaggerated bardic robes and wearing a parody of the Steward's mask. Her song is also a parody—of, among other things, the romantic experience of *Sehnsucht* (bk. 3, chap. 1). Lewis says, in an unpublished letter, that he is satirizing the early Edith Sitwell in this passage.[1]

On the other hand, some of John's adventures in the book are certainly those of "Jack" Lewis. In the second chapter, John sees a vision of a green woodland, with primroses, and hears a musical tone and a voice calling "Come"; beyond the wood, he imagines after the vision is over, is a sea and in it an island (bk. 1, chap. 2). In other words, the island he searches for through most of the book is what his imagination can shape out of an experience that is not in images at all. This, of course, is a description of the experience of *Sehnsucht,* or romantic longing, which Lewis calls *joy* in *Surprised by Joy* and "Romanticism" in the subtitle of this volume. Later in *The Pilgrim's Regress,* the philosophical discussions in the House of Wisdom (bk. 7, chap. 7–bk. 8, chap. 1) reflect Lewis's own intellectual movement "from 'popular realism' to Philosophical Idealism; from Idealism to Pantheism; from Pantheism to Theism; and from Theism to Christianity" (preface); and the biographical pattern of John having to return to his starting place in Puritania reflects Lewis's return, at age 33, to the faith he lost in his early teens.

Since John's early adventures, after leaving home, are the simplest and most easily understood part of the volume, they will be omitted here. The fornication with the brown girl, referred to by Nevill Coghill in the previous chapter, and an affair with Media Halfways (both substitutes for *Sehnsucht*), and an elaborate (and imagistically mixed) attack on Freudianism, take up much of this space. At any rate, John and a walking companion, Vertue—the romantic and the moralist—reach the end of the road to the west at a canyon, which stands for Original Sin; presumably this means that in the world, outside of Christianity, there is no way to overcome one's limits, that all other quests are futile. After a trip north along the canyon, John and Vertue turn south and come to the House of Wisdom. They find there such thinkers as Karl Marx, Herbert Spenser, Benedict Spinoza, Rudolph Steiner (the great influence on

Owen Barfield), Immanuel Kant, and Bernard Bosanquet. Lewis indicates that their food (ideas) is imported—what sustains them is other than the strict philosophic virtues they profess.

The arguments of Wisdom—the father of these philosophers who *does* eat only his own food—in book 7 follow a usual pattern for the later Lewis. There are certain things in the world that cannot be explained as products of the world: in this allegory, the roads of the country, the landlord's (God's) and each man's inner rules, and the island in the West seen by John. Therefore, the universe must be ultimately mental, not physical, for parts of it cannot be explained physically (cf. SJ, chap. 13). According to the headnote of the 1943 edition, the roads stand for logical categories (it does not seem the best symbolism) and the rules for moral values. The island, of course, is a symbol for *Sehnsucht*. This is parallel to the first of the arguments outlined in *Surprised by Joy* for Lewis's conversion from atheism (materialism) to theism (SJ, chap. 13; also, for *Sehnsucht,* chap. 14). The argument from "rules," from moral values perceived by men but not made by them—in short, from natural law—is the basis of two of Lewis's philosophic works; the argument from reason (logical categories) is used in *Miracles*.

John and Vertue take Wisdom's argument in opposite ways, according to their psychologies. John wants to embrace the world as being symbolic of the Spirit (a type of romantic pantheism); Vertue wants to reject the physical world in order to purify his soul. Since Lewis held both romantic and moral positions, this sounds like a split personality; but John, the view-point character, has not yet accepted the rules.

Later, John, in asking help from the eternal Spirit of the philosophers while going along a narrow path on the canyon wall, turns his pantheism into theism (bk. 8, chap. 3; cf. SJ, chap. 14), for a disinterested Spirit cannot give help and a theistic God can. When this position is combined with natural law—the "rules"—John takes the last step into a moral theism (bk. 8, chap. 5).

Two other interesting discussions appear in the book. On the way along the canyon side (moving toward Christianity), John meets a hermit named History, and John is told that the Landlord (God) sends various sorts of messages into the world: the rules to the shepherd-people who could read (the Jews), and various sorts of pictures to the pagans who could not read—pictures of a greater people (the myths of gods), the image of a lady (courtly love in the

Middle Ages), the image of real nature (romantic nature "worship"), and John's island (bk. 8, chaps. 8–10). The Middle Ages are pagan in the sense that the Germanic conquerers in the Dark Ages were; the hermit rather condenses the process at this point. Dante is referred to as the one person who fully understood what the image of the lady implied—which is important both for emphasis on Dante and in contrast to the adulterous emphasis in French courtly love in *The Allegory of Love*.

The second discussion appears after John and Vertue have become Christians, having been baptized (they dive into a river) and undergoing a mystical death with Christ in the process (they come up from their dives inside a cavern and travel out) (bk. 9, chaps. 4–5). Wisdom appears to John in the cavern—presumably not Wisdom himself, as met earlier, but Wisdom as a symbol for the thoughts he embodied—and he says that no one could reach the place John had, that his journey is figurative or mythological. A Voice (God's voice) replies, saying it is not fact but true myth, His mythology. The Voice, evidently as an indication of what is meant by His mythology, thereafter asks whether there were any men, any time, any place, who did not know that grain and wine were a dying-and-yet-living god's body and blood. Thus, the narrative is both mythic (a sacramental death) and argumentative. The latter— the question about the pagan mystery rites, with the grain god resurrected in the spring—suggests that the pagan gods reflect Jesus, and therefore have some truth to them. This is the argument presented to Lewis by Tolkien and Dyson nine days before his conversion: Lewis responded to dying and resurrected gods in myths; in Christ he could turn to their historic model. Christ is the archetype, and the others are the ectypes, foreshadowing the truth or imitating it afterwards. (Simply as an image of temptation in a cavern journey, without the same allegorical level, Psyche is seen in *Till We Have Faces* in a picture near the end undergoing temptations by those whom she has known in this world, as John is here by Wisdom.)

The rest of the book can be briefly indicated: in the land beyond Original Sin, John and Vertue go to the western end of the round world, they see across the water to the west the shape of the mountains that lie to the east of John's birthplace (this is John's "island" he sees across the water), and then—because there are no boats— they must turn around and walk back around the world to reach the mountains (God's home). In other words, John's romantic quest for an island proves to be a confused quest for Heaven. When they return through the fallen world, seeing it with the eyes of faith, they see only ice north of the main road, swamps and jungle south of it. The one exception is a small island of willow trees amid the swamps where the House of Wisdom had been: on it are a few men, but not the sons of wisdom who ate of other food; the angel guide of John and Vertue refers to it as Limbo. This is presumably an adaptation of Dante's Limbo, which is given the only light in Hell. Lewis's Limbo holds those who spend their lives in desire of the Spirit (God) but do not seek to fulfill the desire, and so receive an eternity of unconsummated desire.

The two opposites—ice and swamp—are typical of Lewis's imagination, which often works in terms of either/or. (It is unusual when, in the narrative poem "The Queen of Drum," he offers three roads—but there he is imitating a folk ballad, "Thomas Rymer.") The images of the mountains for Heaven arose from the longed-for Castlereagh Hills Lewis saw from his nursery window as a child (SJ, chap. 1). These holy mountains (Bunyan's Delectable Mountains in *Pilgrim's Progress* are not images of desire) reappear in several of Lewis's fictions—*Out of the Silent Planet*, *The Great Divorce*, *The Voyage of the "Dawn Treader*," and *Till We Have Faces*. Indeed, the number of motifs and ideas in *The Pilgrim's Regress* that reappear in Lewis's later works indicates both how quickly his ideas matured and how little they changed.

Surprised by Joy (1955)

Twenty-two years after the allegorical reshaping of his return to Christianity, Lewis retold his story more directly, as *Surprised by Joy: The Shape of My Early Life*. Instead of a journey, it is a history of Christian faith, apostasy, and a return to faith. Northrop Frye defines a *confession* (in his critical use of the term) as a type of prose fiction or quasi-fiction in which the main character has a significant interest in religion, politics, or art, and the narrative tells of his coming to intellectual terms with his subject.[2] St. Augustine's *Confessions* are an example. In the case of Lewis's work, his "confession" is not of a sensational sort; but he is concerned to show how *Sehnsucht* eventually led him to God. He does not stress to the same extent natural law or reason as supernatural guides.

In the brief preface, Lewis limits the book to tracing the background of his reconversion to Christianity at age 32. This is the structural pattern of the book. Near the end of the volume, he spends a page (chap. 14) listing what he will not tell about his life shortly before his conversion, including his father's death. But this is typical of the whole book: an early vacation in Normandy is not recounted because it did not affect his later life (chap. 1). Several anecdotes about his experiences in World War I are given in brief summary as essentially insignificant (chap. 13), while the story of how he got out the wrong side of the railway station, on first visiting Oxford, walked into the suburb of Botley before realizing his mistake, turning about, and returning is given an elaborate paragraph (chap. 12) because it is an allegory of his life pattern: the pilgrim's regress.

There is a large degree of intellectual shaping in the work. Typical phrases are these: "I must restrain myself. I could continue to describe Oldie for many pages" (chap. 2); "I was already desperately anxious to get rid of my religion; and that for a reason *worth recording*" (chap. 4, stress added). And these on patterns he discovered in his life: "To speak of my nearest relatives is to remind myself how the contrast of Lewis [his father, emotionalism] and Hamilton [his mother, control] dominated my early life" (chap. 3); "The old pattern [of joyful holidays followed by expected disaster] began to repeat itself" (chap. 12).

In addition to this shaping of his past for artistic purposes, there is also a fictionalizing effect from Lewis's use of pseudonyms for various personages and places: Belsen, for Wynyard School; Oldie, for Robert Capron; Wee Wee, for Capron's son (chap. 2); Mountbracken, for Glenmacken, a house (chap. 3); Chartres, for Cherbourg School; Wyvern College, for Malvern College; Tubbs, for Arthur C. Allen, headmaster at Cherbourg; Sirrah and Pogo, for teachers at Cherbourg (chap. 4); Fribble, Borage, Parsley, etc., for various fellow students at Malvern (chap. 7). Also, at least six persons are identified only by one or more initials.

Other devices accompany this fictional tone. An extreme example of concrete detail is found at the beginning of chapter 2: "Clop-clop-clop-clop . . . we are in a four-wheeler rattling over the uneven squaresets of a Belfast street through the damp twilight of a September evening, 1908" (Lewis's ellipse). Not only are the senses of hearing and touch ("damp") appealed to, but the historical present tense is used. Lewis creates the immediacy of his material for his reader—no doubt in part because he had a far more vivid, imagistic memory than most people.

An analysis of one chapter—the fifth, "Renaissance"—will complete this discussion. The chapter begins with an elaborate comparison of the popular idea of a classical rebirth after the Middle Ages with a person's emotional rebirth after puberty, a rebirth that brings back to life many of the interests of childhood that were lost during the later stage of boyhood. Whether this is universally true is doubtful, but Lewis is illustrating his pattern. (It also ties to the critics' comments about Lewis's "immaturity" that were mentioned in the last chapter.)

The narrative begins with the moment of Lewis's discovery of Wagner's Ring Cycle through an Arthur Rackham illustration. With the discovery came a renewed love for Northernness and the renewed call of *Sehnsucht*. The next few pages trace Lewis's purchase of Wagnerian records and other materials tied to Northernness; then follow four paragraph-long points about the significance of this love, including a resulting love of external nature as Lewis looked for—at first—Wagnerian scenes.

At this juncture an odd thing occurs: by means of a casual transition, Lewis shifts to the history of his early fantasy world, Animal-Land (now combined with his brother's imaginary India to produce Boxen), first mentioned in the first chapter of *Surprised by Joy*. He describes several of the characters, some resembling his and his brother's position in relationship to their father, but others, earlier in creation, not tied to anything the brothers were experiencing. After two long paragraphs on the Boxonian world, Lewis cuts off the train of reminiscences, saying his only reason for mentioning it was to indicate his early imaginative life. He adds a paragraph to the effect that belief, in a religious sense, entered into neither his love of Northernness nor the Boxonian society. And he brings the material back to the nonimaginative world in a final paragraph in which he wins a scholarship to "Wyvern" College in 1913.

This chapter shows less chronology than most, but some characteristics are apparent. The analogy at the beginning is an inventive way to start—not as dramatic as the "clop-clop-clop-clop" of the second chapter, but, for an educated audience, a clever gambit. The importance of the experience of Northernness, through Rackham's picture, is brought home in a simile:

It was as if the Arctic itself, all the deep layers of secular ice, should change not in a week nor in an hour, but instantly, into a landscape of grass and primroses and orchards in bloom, deafened with bird songs and astir with running water. (Chap. 5)

Perhaps, however, a changing of the Arctic into a British landscape is not the perfect simile for a desire for Northernness—surely, a change of (say) Irish greenness into Icelandic spareness would be more appropriate. This is not just quibbling. In several places Lewis defended use of common images. For example, in a poem titled "A Confession" (1954) he attacks T. S. Eliot's comparison of an evening to an etherized patient in "The Love Song of J. Alfred Prufrock." Lewis's Arctic simile is one aimed at making a moment's importance meaningful to a large audience for whom flowers are more valuable than ice. One need not judge Lewis at all hypocritical in use of such a simile: for him, writing was meant to communicate. And he does offer on the same page an imagistic description of Northernness: "a vision of huge, clear spaces hanging above the Atlantic in the endless twilight of Northern summer, remoteness, severity." But the choice of the direction of the change in the simile does indicate why Lewis was a popular writer (in a good sense), not a belletristic essayist.

Other aspects of the rest of the chapter are typical of Lewis. The ennumerated list of four results of the return of Northernness shows his methodical, perhaps scholarly, make-up. The comparison of Lord Big (one of the Boxonian characters, a frog) with Sir Winston Churchill brings the Boxonian to life, as does—to a narrower extent—the comparison of Lieutenant James Bar (a brown bear) with John Betjeman (later poet laureate, who was one of Lewis's first tutees at Oxford). Probably the only limitation on the chapter is that it has less moralizing than most chapters (despite some critics, the present age seems to read as much moral advice—of various sorts—as has any age) and less wit and humor than some.

As noted earlier, the introduction of Boxen into Lewis's narrative is odd. Lewis states that his inner life of Joy becomes, after the returned love of Northernness, entirely separate from his outer life—and that even Animal-Land, imaginative as it was, belonged to the outer life. Lewis then begins a partial history of Boxen. As indicated, he *does* defend it later as part of his imaginative life in 1911 and 1912. But Boxen is not part of his "rebirth" as announced in the chapter title, "Renaissance." That has to do with Wagner, Norse myths, and Joy. Boxen has all the signs of being a casually added passage, interesting as part of Lewis's background as a creative writer but hardly necessary as part of his conversion. No one who enjoys Lewis's books would want the passage omitted, but it is hard to defend as germane to his theme.

Lewis's book as a whole shows the same pattern. In a book of fifteen chapters, why are two spent on Lewis's one year at an English public school? That he was a misfit is obvious, but he seems to be reacting to all the British propaganda in favor of public school education—and in a very defensive manner. The first of these chapters, the sixth, "Bloodery," describes the social hierarchy at the school, the "fagging" of the younger boys, the homosexuality, and the emphasis on sports. (Of these, homosexuality comes off lightest in Lewis's treatment.) In the next chapter, "Light and Shade," in addition to praise for one teacher and the school library, Lewis indicates the system's failure, so far as he was concerned, because he became a prig. In short, Lewis seems occasionally to wander from his thesis—the tracing of his conversion—when a marginal subject has enough emotional power of either a positive (Boxen) or a negative sort (the British public schools). It makes *Surprised by Joy* a more human and—for many readers—a more interesting volume.

A Grief Observed (1961)

Turning from *The Pilgrim's Regress* to *Surprised by Joy* may be something like turning from *The Pilgrim's Progress* to *Grace Abounding,* but there is no analogy in Bunyan for Lewis's third autobiographical volume. Perhaps *A Grief Observed* can be said to be a shorter, prose, more orthodox *In Memoriam.*

About the time of *Surprised by Joy* in 1955, Lewis was surprised by a different Joy—Helen Joy Davidman, divorced from William Lindsay Gresham and the mother of two boys. She had begun writing to Lewis about the time of her conversion to Christianity in 1948; she first visited him in 1952; she returned to England at the time of her divorce in 1954 (Gresham was living with another woman); and she and Lewis were married in 1956 legally and in 1957 religiously (the latter before she was taken from a hospital to Lewis's home, the Kilns). She had a remission of her cancer for a few years, but it returned and she died in 1960. The next year, under the pseudonym of N. W. Clerk, Lewis published *A Grief Observed.*

The book is divided by Roman numerals into four sections, and the reader learns at the beginning of the fourth that these represent four empty notebooks found in the house after his wife's death in which the writer has been recording his feelings. He also at this point reveals his dual purpose: to write as a release mechanism against collapse and to describe the state of grief. The first has been successful; the second, unsuccessful, for grief has turned out not to be some limited types of feelings but a process. Further, he notes soon after, the process itself has not been recorded very successfully, for changes have already started before he has been aware of them.

The form that the book takes is a series of jottings—presumably one or two made per day—printed as separate paragraphs. (There are thirty-one in the first notebook, thirty-three in the second, forty-eight in the third, and forty in the fourth; there is also much variation in the length of entries.) The effect is something like Blaise Pascal's *Pensées*. Some of the shorter entries are nicely epigrammatic: "Talk to me about the truth of religion and I'll listen gladly. Talk to me about the duty of religion and I'll listen submissively. But don't come talking to me about the consolations of religion or I shall suspect that you don't understand" (nbk. 2).

The reason for publication, not just writing—besides the overall progress recorded in returning to the Christian faith—is perhaps best indicated by the opening of one of the paragraphs: "No one ever told me that grief . . ." (nbk. 1). Lewis has captured a process in life that—outside of Tennyson—has had few recorders; for others in grief to learn that their reactions are not excessive, that another has journeyed through the same emotional problems, is reassuring.

Time references in the series are vague. The second notebook was begun less than a month after the wife's death. A week passes between a comment on God as the cosmic sadist in the second notebook and a calmer analysis of the emotional causes for the outburst in the third. But the process itself seems more important than the time it takes.

How much, if any, fictionalizing there is in this volume is uncertain. Probably there is some. Lewis speaks of being "at the club" (nbk. 1)—which probably, for a British reader, gives an effect of a Londoner writing. The inability of the narrator to recall a specific ballad or folktale in which the dead complain that mourning bothers them (nbk. 3) sounds more like an average memory rather than Lewis's. The children (nbk. 1) are not identified as step-children.

Two of the comparisons come from mathematics: solid geometry (nbk. 2) and quadratic equations (nbk. 3). Also, for a work by Lewis, there are very few references to nature and very few quotations (with no authors mentioned). Although these examples suggest a slight fictionalization of the persona—perhaps to avoid identification—no one knows enough of Lewis's private feelings to say if some of the reactions reported in the book are exaggerated or invented, or enough of his private life to say if he really wrote the book over a period of no more than two months in four notebooks. But the usual assumption is that the reactions are not exaggerated and the writing process is veritable, allowing for revisions; otherwise, why not publish the book under his own name with an introductory note saying it was largely fiction?

Certainly some of the images and ideas are not fictional. The use of H. throughout for his wife refers to Joy Davidman's first name, Helen. The effect of Charles Williams's death (without his name being mentioned) is described (nbk. 1) as Lewis describes it in letters.[3] The anecdote of H. putting off a request from God, only to learn He wanted to give her a feeling of joy (nbk. 3), is told in letters.[4] The joke that, if God had wanted people to live as lilies of the field, He should have given people their constitution (nbk. 4), is also used in letters (LAL, 20, 21, 76). Most specifically, in a letter to Mary Willis Shelburne (LAL, 89), Lewis discusses his grief over Joy's death, using the image of sorrow as a winding road, revealing new landscapes at each turn, that he also uses in *A Grief Observed* as a winding valley (nbk. 4). He says in the same letter that he feels closest to Joy when he mourns her least, which is also a realization that he uses in the book (nbk. 3). Since Davidman died on 13 July 1960, and this letter was written on 24 September, the two months since her death obviously have given Lewis much of his content (the winding valley image is at the beginning of the fourth notebook).

As with *In Memoriam,* the literary structure is partly one of balance and partly one of groupage. Probably the most famous balance in *In Memoriam* is that of the two door lyrics (nos. 7 and 119) that almost frame the whole poem. *A Grief Observed* is shorter and has nothing that spectacular, but, for one example, Lewis worries in the last paragraph of the first notebook that he has no photograph of H. that is any good and he cannot picture her clearly in his mind, and he suggests a psychological reason for the latter; then, in the fourth notebook, he spends several paragraphs on the dangers, for him, of images, beginning from photographs and memories and noting how real people, including wives, continually shatter one's image of them. Part of this latter discussion is also at a religious level, in that it describes God as the great iconoclast who continually breaks down false images of Himself.

In *In Memoriam,* there are several sequences of lyrics connected by images and ideas, such as the ship lyrics near the beginning (nos. 9–17). A sequence of images in *A Grief Observed* that is quite effective is that of the house of cards (nbks. 3–4). At first the image is that of a collapse of a house of cards—the writer's faith being imagination and his love, egotism. He agrees this sort of card castle should collapse, and he fears a restoration of faith that is just a new card castle. Later, he sees that the only way God had to show that his faith was as weak as a house of cards was to knock it down. Finally, he realizes that God will continue to knock down his buildings of cards until he discovers reality—or is given up as hopeless. The repetition with slight modifications through these images is much like the repetition in a lyric sequence—Shakespeare's variations on immortality-through-poetry in his sonnets, Petrarch's puns on *laurel* in his poems to Laura, or Tennyson's modifications of Christmas celebrations in *In Memoriam* (although the latter is also a time-sequencing device).

There are other resemblances to *In Memoriam:* Lewis worries about the possible morbidity of writing down his grief (nbk. 1), as Tennyson worries about his overemphasis on grief (lyric 5); Lewis speaks of reaching out for the real, beyond the products of imagination (nbk. 4), as Tennyson writes of groping beyond nature for the divine (lyric 55). But these are probably all accidental resemblances, arising from similar materials. More significant to the understanding of Lewis's mind is the Dantean quotation used as the last sentence of *A Grief Observed.* In identifying H. as she died with Beatrice as she turned her eyes from Dante to God, Lewis is establishing the Christian hierarchy. Human loves are very important, but the love of God is even more so.

Chapter Three
The Literary and Lexical Historian

C. S. Lewis writes in *An Experiment in Criticism* that, after editors, textbook critics, lexicographers, and the like, he has owed most to

that despised class, the literary historians. . . . These have helped, first of all, by telling me what works exist. But still more by putting them in their setting; thus showing me what demands they were meant to satisfy, what furniture they presupposed in the minds of their readers. (chap. 11)

Thus, it is no wonder that Lewis himself turned to writing literary histories. *The Allegory of Love* (1936) and *English Literature in the Sixteenth Century, excluding Drama* (1954)—the latter volume in the Oxford History of English Literature—are examples of different types of literary histories: the first traces the development of a genre, the allegorical narrative about love, through the centuries; the second is one century's literary cross section.

To these are added two other volumes in this chapter. *Studies in Words* (1960, 1967) is a group of essays on words, almost every essay tracing the development of a word or associated words through the centuries. Lewis says in his introduction that his interest grew out of his study of literature. *The Discarded Image* (1964) is again a cross section, not of a literary period but of the medieval world view. This fits the above description of a literary historian explaining what "furniture" literary works "presupposed" in their original readers' (or auditors') minds.

Of course, Lewis himself is not entirely objective in these works. He does things such as calling the plain style "Drab" in his sixteenth-century volume—obviously, a loaded term. (The common reader will not get excited over diction, but critics did; other biases extend beyond the field of literature itself.) Partly Lewis just was doing what writers traditionally have done—that is, expressing opinions—partly he was showing his delight in argument by stirring up controversy. Even the book on words has some argumentative points made rather indirectly.

Why did Lewis believe in literary histories? It was more than has been said. Lewis writes in his introductory lecture as a professor at Cambridge University: "to study the past does indeed liberate us from the present, from the idols of our own market-place. . . . The unhistorical are usually, without knowing it, enslaved to a fairly recent past" (*"De Descriptione Temporum,"* 1954). Thus literary histories are an aid—in addition to the literature itself—in freeing oneself from a dominance by whatever is the current "truth" in literature, whether it be realism, naturalism, postrealism—or fantasies by Tolkien and Lewis. Other people in the past, with tastes no worse than one's own—simply different—have enjoyed other types of writings. Of course, for Lewis, romantic as he started and conservative as he became, there was often an assumption that it was especially wise to be liberated from the views of the twentieth century. But that bias does not destroy the organized information his histories contain.

The Allegory of Love (1936, rev. 1938)

Lewis made his reputation as a historical critic with *The Allegory of Love* and never returned to its topic again in any substantial way. Later writers have raised questions about aspects of the book, but no one has denied that it established a whole field (or perhaps two fields) of critical understanding in English.

Lewis's two topics in the book are courtly love and erotic allegory. He spends his first chapter defining and exemplifying courtly love (several later writers find flaws here); his second chapter traces the historical development of allegory from classical times as a popular form (this material has not been challenged). At this point his two topics come together, and he spends the third chapter on a French combination, one of the major medieval poems: *The Romance of the Rose*. Then Lewis turns to the English poems in the tradition of the *Roman de la rose* for his last four chapters; these concern primarily Chaucer's *Troilus and Criseyde,* John Gower's *Confessio Amantis,* Thomas Usk's *Testament of Love,* a number of minor works in the fifteenth and early sixteenth centuries, and Edmund Spenser's *Faerie Queene.* (Only brief passages in these later chapters have been challenged.)

It is, by the way, in connection with *Troilus and Criseyde* that Lewis's male chauvinism shows itself; he writes of Criseyde's fall after her return to the Greek side in the Trojan War: "all men, and all good women, will hate Diomede" (chap. 4, sec. 2). Will not *some* men admire this seducer? But it is only one slip in a long book.

It would take too long to trace all of the attacks on or questions about parts of this book, and it is not necessary since they can be found summarized in a checklist of Lewisian secondary materials listed in the bibliography. Those positions most often or most strongly attacked are Lewis's development of the Coleridgean distinction between allegory and symbolism, his belief that courtly love was one of the three or four real changes in human sentiment on record, his inclusion of adultery in the four marks of courtly love, his acceptance of Andreas Capellanus's *De Arte Honeste Amandi* as straight-forward exposition, his rather romantic reading of Gower's *Confessio Amantis,* and (with a tendency more toward modification than rejection) his contrast between the Bower of Bliss and the Garden of Adonis in *The Faerie Queene.* To these may be added a major flaw in his organization: Lewis omits *The Canterbury Tales* as besides his thesis (chap. 4, sec. 2), although G. K. Kittridge's seminal 1912 essay, "Chaucer's Discussion of Marriage," had already shown the development of the poem of courtly-love *marriage* in "The Franklin's Tale" before *The Kings Quair,* which Lewis celebrates for this feat (chap. 6, sec. 2). It is true that "The Franklin's Tale" is not allegorical—which probably is what Lewis means by it being outside his thesis—but neither is *Troilus and Criseyde,* which he does discuss. Indeed, Lewis's passing reference to "The Franklin's Tale" (chap. 3, sec. 5) suggests that he sees the implications of the story but avoids an adequate development. The charge here is one of weak thematic organization, not dishonesty: Lewis is not consistent in avoiding or discussing nonallegorical works.

For a student of Lewis, rather than a student of medieval love allegory, this volume contains many personal marks. For example, in Lewis's discussion of Spenser, he cites Spenser's listing of Eros, Storge, and Philia as the three kinds of love (chap. 7, sec. 3): with the addition of agape, these are the terms for Lewis's *The Four Loves.* And Lewis shows touches of his gift for philia in this book: surely the reference to "orcs" (chap. 7, sec. 1) is the first published citation of J. R. R. Tolkien's creatures of Middle-earth, even though, in context, it might get by as a shortened use of the Anglo-Saxon *orcneas* ("hell-corpses") in *Beowulf*. Possibly the military "officer of [Lewis's] acquaintance" (chap. 7, sec. 3) was his brother. And the book is dedicated to Owen Barfield.

Other echoes of past or future writings appear. An allusion to Aengus (chap. 7, sec. 3) may remind a reader of a lyric about that Irish god in *Spirits in Bondage*. The reference to a man who wrote an "apologetic allegory" of a general nature and found himself praised or blamed for writing a defense of Roman Catholicism (chap. 7, sec. 3) probably refers to Lewis's troubles over readers' identifications of Puritania and Mother Kirk in *The Pilgrim's Regress*; also, Lewis's reference to escaping the prison of the *Zeitgeist* (chap. 2, sec. 6) is a brief parallel to the episode in the earlier book in which John escapes the dungeon of the Spirit of the Age (*Pilgrim's Regress,* bk. 3, chap. 9).

Lewis's mention of the Renaissance not being of great significance in the context of his book (chap. 6, sec. 4) is only a mild touch of his later attack on the significance of that period in his introduction to *English Literature in the Sixteenth Century*. His brief footnote on the development of the meanings of *frank* (chap. 3, sec. 2) may be considered a casual foretaste of his chapter on *free, frank,* and related words in *Studies in Words*. Occasionally, Lewis does something in this volume that he will attack later, as in his derivation of the King and Queen of Love from forgotten fertility rites (chap. 3, sec. 2): the very thing he decries in literary criticism—with, however, a concluding irony—in "The Anthropological Approach" (1962). Finally, tying this book to most of Lewis's other books, a reader may notice the twenty-two references to Dante listed in the index. Colin Hardie, in "Dante and the Tradition of Courtly Love" (1966), surveys Lewis's more significant reference to Dante in *The Allegory of Love,* disagreeing with Lewis at points.[1] But the number of references is more significant here. Lewis at one point compares the organizations of Dante and Jean de Meun and concludes, "Dante remains a strong candidate for the supreme poetical honours of the world" (chap. 3, sec. 5).

The book is also interesting for Lewis's general pronouncements on literature. No doubt this tendency was encouraged by Lewis's early readings of Boswell's *Life of Johnson* (SJ, 136); but if its father was Johnson, its mother was Lewis's own need to set up rules for his writing. (His later books of literary history and criticism do not have so many pronouncements.) These are matters like Lewis's dis-

cussion of literary unity of the highest order, referring to a work
with "the greatest diversity of subordinated detail" (chap. 3, sec.
4, with Dante as an example); a definition of the plain style (not
yet called Drab), romantic writing as bridging the conscious and
unconscious minds, an imitation of general human nature as also
catching individual nature (many of Lewis's examples in his religious
books are in this eighteenth-century approach), and meaning in
good literature as beyond the author's intentions (all chap. 5, sec.
1); the dominant literary form of an age attracting authors whose
strengths are elsewhere (chap. 6, sec. 1, with George MacDonald
as an example); a "law of literary history" that a potentially great
writer can only become so if he can find the appropriate form for
his genius (chap. 6, sec. 4); "the Wordsworthian heresy" of common
diction (chap. 6, sec. 5); the reader's proper attention to the imaginative tone of a poem (chap. 6, sec. 6); and the variety of imaginative quality possible within a genre (chap. 7, sec. 2, as Lewis
would demonstrate of the epic in A Preface to "Paradise Lost")—this
last passage foreruns the dislike of depreciatory criticism found at
the end of Lewis's career in An Experiment in Criticism.

No doubt a different critic could make a list of moral statements
by Lewis, or statements on society or the relationships between the
sexes; but these possibilities, as well as the above list, only suggest
the richness of The Allegory of Love beyond its nominal topic. And
it is a positive book: Lewis praises more than he damns. Few books
on what seems such a remote subject are such lively general reading.

English Literature in the Sixteenth Century, Excluding Drama (1954)

Eighteen years after his first literary history, Lewis produced his
second and better (if less influential) work in the field. English
Literature in the Sixteenth Century may not have the brilliance of
(scholarly) youth, and it certainly cannot claim to be introducing
readers to essentially a new field as The Allegory of Love could, but
its scholarship has held up more successfully than has its predeces-
sor's treatment of courtly love, and it has maturity beyond the earlier
work in being more constantly focused on its topic.

The organization of a literary history is, in general, chronological.
After his introduction, "New Learning and New Ignorance," Lewis's
book 1, "Late Medieval," covers approximately the first half of the

century in Scotland (which had good poetry at the time) and England (which had poor). Book 2, " 'Drab,' " covering works of religious controversy in addition to poetry and other prose, overlaps in period with the first book, running from the teens of the century into the seventies and eighties. Book 3, " 'Golden,' " covers Sidney and Spenser as well as other prose and verse, including Shakespeare's sonnets, and it does not overlap as much, beginning in the 1570s and finishing the century. Lewis has an epilogue, "New Tendencies," that treats, among other things, of the development of the metaphysical verse as a Silver Age following the Golden.

When this volume was first published, the reviewers saw three major aspects that were (and are) controversial. One that does not bulk large in Lewis's text, for obvious reasons, is the avoidance of the term *Renaissance*. In two pages of his introduction, Lewis indicates the looseness of the term and its loaded nature. Lewis's refusal to call the sixteenth century the English Renaissance, however, carries with it implications of a denial of traditional views of the general "re-birth" in the period. The second, and related, aspect is Lewis's attack on the humanists of the time; he spends fourteen pages of his introduction essentially in an attack, although he praises their editing of texts, and the rest of the book has numerous negative comments. Helen Gardner is moved to complain that the introduction

is devoted to proving by skillfully selected quotation and a complete refusal of imaginative sympathy that Humanism was inhumane and that the Humanists . . . did "immense harm." . . . The references [to Erasmus] are nearly all derogatory. It is never suggested that reforms in education, and the Humanist insistence on the aesthetic merits of ancient literature, could have any connection with the appearance of our "Golden Age."[2]

The third controversial aspect is the use of the terms "Drab" and "Golden" in reference to the poetry. Lewis protests near the end of his introduction, "*Drab* is not used as a dyslogistic term. It marks a period in which, for good or ill, poetry has little richness either of sound or images. The good work is neat and temperate, the bad flat and dry. There is more bad than good." But what if he had called it "spoken (or colloquial) verse" or simply "the plain style"? That would have avoided the pejorative connotations of *Drab*. Likewise, Lewis protests about *Golden*: "The epithet *golden* is not eulogistic. By *golden* poetry I mean not simply good poetry, but poetry which is, so to speak, innocent or ingenuous." When Lewis lists three characteristics of golden poetry, they are a peculiar lot: (1) it avoids some meters (the poulter's measure and fourteeners) and seldom uses others (stanzas in octosyllabic lines, alternate octosyllabic and hexasyllabic lines); in general, it avoids becoming repetitious in its forms; (2) its language is free, borrowing from popular phraseology; and (3) its imagery often refers to external nature (bk. 3, chap. 3, sec. 3). Lewis seems to be describing a simple, nondidactic lyricism. But because Lewis's terms are loaded (despite his protests), they help the liveliness of his book.

It would be easy to multiply examples of odd minor judgments in this literary history, beyond those pointed out by reviewers. Lewis discusses Robert Southwell's poetry (epilogue, sec. 2) without ever mentioning his most famous lyric, "The Burning Babe." His panegyric and discussion of the poetry of Thomas Campion (epilogue, sec. 3) does not make distinctions that one would expect—for example, the seriousness of the songs in *The Third* and the lightness of those in the *Fourth Book of Ayrs*.[3] Nor does he try to place any of the lyrics in connection to Campion's life, but that avoidance might be expected of the writer who attacked "the personal heresy."

But what is more interesting is what Lewis *does* say about Campion. Besides some discussion of the first four poems in *A Book of Ayres* to show Campion's variety in content, Lewis spends much of his space on versification: an imitation of some of Horace's metrics in English (not just stresses for long syllables, but long and short syllables according to Latin rules also), various classical feet used in stress patterns, the use of equivalence (a single stress balancing a metrical foot in other lines), etc. Indeed, a reader soon realizes how typical this is of the book: there is a traditionalist's Rules of Prosody buried in Lewis's comments. He discusses the late medieval meter and Skeltonics (bk. 1, chap. 2, sec. 1), Sir Thomas Wyatt's versification (bk. 2, chap. 2); he has running complaints against the poulter's measure (also bk. 2, chap. 2); he offers some comments on theories and examples of classical prosody (bk. 3, chap. 1), on the versification used in satires (bk. 3, chap. 3, sec. 2), on Simpsonian rhyme, on failures in sonnets' versification (e.g., in Barnaby Barnes's *Parthenophil and Parthenophe*), on versification and structure of sonnets—stanza forms have always been part of prosody—in Shakespeare's sequence (all bk. 3, chap. 3, sec. 3); and he makes a final comparison of Drab, Golden, and Metaphysical (or at least

Donnean) metrics (epilogue, sec. 2). All of these (and there are many more comments) are a reminder of the lectures that Oxford University missed when it elected C. Day Lewis as Professor of Poetry over C. S. Lewis in 1950.

There are many virtues to *English Literature in the Sixteenth Century* that have not been touched on—the often-praised section on Scottish poets, Lewis's ability to write about theological works in terms of their literary merits, and his skill at praising the good works in varied ways (it is always more easy to depreciate than to praise). But in terms of Lewis's career, the autobiographical touches are of major interest here. As was suggested earlier, they are less apparent in this book than in *The Allegory of Love*. For example, the references to the Inklings are minor: J. A. W. Bennett and H. V. D. Dyson are thanked "for advice and criticism" in the preface, and Charles Williams is noted as a good ode writer (bk. 3, chap. 1); but there is not an equivalent to Tolkien's "orcs" here—unless the analogy of the painter with one major work and several minor works (bk. 3, chap. 1) was built on Tolkien's "Leaf by Niggle" and so carries a parallel of Tolkien to Spenser.

This chapter—"Sidney and Spenser"—also discusses, with a "merest conjecture," the influence of Ireland's nature on Edmund Spenser: Lewis quotes Bernard Shaw on the Irish-nature-caused "never satisfying dreaming." Lewis then wonders if that was why Spenser sent Prince Arthur, without literary authority, on his endless quest, and he concludes, in words that apply to himself as well as (probably better than) to Spenser: "To a Christian Platonist these formless longings would logically appear as among the sanest and most fruitful experiences we have; for their object really exists and really draws us to itself." This is the call of *Sehnsucht* that Lewis depicted in *The Pilgrim's Regress* and *Surprised by Joy*.

Further echoes of his other writings may be suggested more briefly. Several religious writers are discussed who base arguments on natural law, as Lewis does in "Right and Wrong" and *The Abolition of Man*; here is part of his background (cf. the discussions of Bracton, Thomas More, Poynet, Richard Hooker). Lewis quotes the passage from David Lindsay's *Monarche* that gave him the title of *That Hideous Strength* (bk. 1, chap. 2, sec. 1) and from John Studley's translation of *Hippolytus* that gave him the name of the Marshwiggle in *The Silver Chair* (bk. 2, chap. 2).[4] Lewis mentions his preference for poetry that focuses on its subject rather than its author (bk. 1, chap.

2, sec. 1)—certainly his bias in *The Personal Heresy*. Even Lewis's nine references to Dante (listed in the index) are subdued to his matter and are mostly trivial in context. Perhaps the most interesting of these minor echoes of Lewis's other concerns is in a discussion of Michael Drayton's first "Nimphall" in *Muses Elizium*: "we are left with two inhuman, inexplicable voices uttering their passion for beauty, and save for that, passionless. It is thus that real fairies . . . would speak if they existed" (bk. 3, chap. 3, sec. 3). This is echoed, with appropriate modifications, in the appearance of the beautiful, passionless God of the Grey Mountain to Orual in *Till We Have Faces* (bk. 1, chap. 15), the romance published two years after this literary history—but in this likeness it is not Drayton influencing Lewis; it is simply a mark of Lewis's sensibility that he would see the nymphs in Drayton's work and would create his own version of God's unchanging nature in terms of beauty beyond passion.

Studies in Words (1960, exp. 1967)

Endowed with a phenomenal memory for the works he read, with a logician's ability at making distinctions, and with a facility in learning and retaining languages; trained in the classics and earlier English literature; in love with literature, Lewis had all the necessary ingredients to be a philologist. Indeed, the Inklings tended in the same direction. Owen Barfield began his authorial career (outside of a children's book and some works in journals) with *History in English Words* (1926) and *Poetic Diction* (1928). Among his later essays are "The Meaning of the Word 'Literal' " (1960) and a small book, *Speaker's Meaning* (1967), which takes its title from a passage in *Studies in Words* (chap. 1, sec. 4).[5] Likewise, Tolkien produced *A Middle English Vocabulary* (1922), "Some Contributions to Middle-English Lexicography" (1925), "The Name 'Nodens' " (1932), " 'Iththlen' in *Sawles Warden*" (1947, in collaboration with S. R. T. O. d'Ardenne), and "Middle English 'Losenger' " (1953).

If the preceding paragraph, with its lists, seems to some readers a dull beginning, it is (if examples of word usage were substituted for book and essay titles) an appropriate one. This volume is probably Lewis's least read ("The readers I have principally in view are students" [chap. 1]) and least used. For example, A. C. Hamilton in his recent annotated edition of *The Faerie Queene* has no note on a passage in which the pains of lovers "seeme gainst common sence to them most sweet" (bk. 4, can. 10, st. 2, l. 4); Lewis finds this *common* to mean not "normal" but "vulgar" (chap. 6, sec. 9). Thus, Lewis asserts, the word does not mean what today's reader means by it: the result is misleading—precisely the sort of point an editor makes for his reader. Of course, Hamilton may not agree with Lewis's reading and so quietly passes it over, but the likelihood is that he has not seen it.[6]

On the other hand, although not popularly written and not greatly influential, Lewis's book does have its virtues for the proper audience. Outside of an introduction and a concluding chapter, "At the Fringe of Language," the book consists in its original form of seven chapters, on "Nature," "Sad," "Wit," "Free," "Sense," "Simple," and "Conscience and Conscious." After Lewis's death, three further essays, intended for a second book of the same type, were added: "World," "Life," and "I Dare Say." The material at its simplest can be seen in the last title. Lewis begins with modern weak meanings of "I dare say," in Dickens's *Bleak House,* W. S. Gilbert's *Mikado,* several children's books by E. Nesbit, and the debate in the House of Lords over publication of Lawrence's *Lady Chatterley's Lover.* In these sources, it means something like "probably" or "possibly." In earlier literature, however, it means something like "I affirm" or "I assert." Lewis gives examples from Sir Thomas Malory's *Morte Darthur,* John Bunyan's *Pilgrim's Progress,* and three novels by Jane Austen. Thus, the modern student has learned to avoid misreading the older usage of "I dare say" by applying the modern meaning.

The other chapters are more complex than this, even though they are normally more chronologically arranged. That on "Nature" has fifteen sections. Part of the complexity is due to Lewis's development of parallels and sometimes influences in other languages, usually classical. The "Nature" discussion runs the various forms of the Greek *phusis* (physicality), Latin *natura* (nature), and Anglo-Saxon *cynd* (kind). Since Lewis's intention is not to trace derivations of words but to follow their shifts in meaning and sentiment, their reflection of cultural ideas (chap. 1), words of related meanings are important for his thesis.

The usefulness of this book to a student of earlier literature is obvious. But there are at least passages that will be of interest to other parts of Lewis's readership. For example, his Christian audience

might well find the chapter on "Conscience and Conscious" interesting, for Lewis traces a change in meaning of *conscience* (Greek
suneidesis) because of some passages in the New Testament in his
sixth section, "The Internal Lawgiver": the word shifts from meaning internal knowledge to meaning internal judgment, while often
retaining its former meaning. Previously the Greek *synteresis* had
been used for the moral judgment. Later the twelfth section, "Conscience as Fear," traces the further shift of conscience into meaning
the fear of damnation, of hellfire. Obviously, it is not just a reading
of earlier literature (including the epistles to the Corinthians and
Romans) that will be improved by this chapter, but also present
religious communications. In addition, the chapter on "World" has
three sections about biblical translation (secs. 4–6) and subsequent
comments on the influence of the (confusing) translations (secs. 7–
8).

Literary critics may learn something about the expression of negative literary judgments from "At the Fringes of Language"; anyone
who loves language and uses it professionally can benefit from Lewis's
introductory discussion of good and bad diction and verbicide, "the
murder of a word"—that is, its meaning (chap. 1; also, on *liberal,*
chap. 5, sec. 6). For an audience curious about Lewis's ideas, the
chapter on "Life" is of particular interest. This chapter is one of
those added to the second edition, and it does not seem to fall quite
under his stated purpose for his book. By the fourth section, Lewis
has moved primarily to modern meanings, and he stays with that
concern throughout most of the rest of the chapter. He wants to
define what F. R. Leavis means by the "study of literature" as "a
discipline of intelligence, fostering life" or D. H. Lawrence means
by "in life [we] have got to live or we are nothing" (sec. 6). Implicitly, not explicitly, Bergson's and Shaw's Life Force comes into
the discussion (secs. 6, 8, 9). In short, Lewis exposes much of the
unconscious vagueness of modern vitalists for whom *life* is a praise
word without traditional meaning. Although Lewis in *Mere Christianity* asks if the Bergson-Shaw beliefs are not "the greatest achievement of wishful thinking the world has yet seen?" (bk. 1, chap.
4), in *Studies in Words* there is no attack, just analysis. Although
in the preface to *The Pilgrim's Regress,* Lewis puts D. H. Lawrence
to the South on his map, as far south as humans have reached—
that is, an exemplum of the irrational, orgiastic, and undisci-
plined—in *Studies in Words* Lewis says of a passage from *Sons and*

Lovers in which a couple, copulating in the woods, feel identified with living objects and are "carried by life" that his, Lewis's concern is with Lawrence's meaning of *life*: "neither moral nor literary criticism has any place in the present inquiry" (sec. 8). Of course Lewis has some fun with the passage—since the couple do not fear pregnancy, they seem to have made previous arrangements not to be carried too far by life—but basically his assertion is true. Perhaps because of the genre of his book (although that would not have stopped the early Lewis) or because his analytic discussion carries its own implicit revelation of the weakness of Leavis's and Lawrence's meanings or because he had learned that attacks were discounted,[7] Lewis's tone in this late book is far from that in his earlier volumes. Helen Gardner has written of the scholarly books published in the days of Lewis's Cambridge professorship. They "were slight works compared with his earlier books; but they were far more balanced and genial in their temper" (Gardner, 428).

This discussion has already led to comparisons between *Studies in Words* and Lewis's life and other works. Briefly, other such details can be mentioned: two references to Irish diction (chap. 4, sec. 1; chap. 7, sec. 2); three uses of Dante, all minor (traceable through the index); no references to any Inklings; one discussion of *world* and *earth* as used in H. G. Wells's *First Men in the Moon,* far from Lewis's imitation of that book in *Out of the Silent Planet* (chap. 9, sec. 9); an anti-humanists comment, as was typical of *English Literature in the Sixteenth Century* (chap. 5, sec. 6); a reference to Jeremy Taylor's quotation of an earlier work that hopes the damned may enjoy a *refrigerium*—the theological basis for *The Great Divorce* (chap. 10, sec. 2); and a discussion that foreshadows *The Discarded Image* on the medieval model of the universe (chap. 10, sec. 2). But the most amusing parallel is not one of content but form. In *Studies in Words,* Lewis uses the term "the *dangerous sense*" of a word to mean the modern dominant sense that is likely to be read back into earlier literature, and he abbreviates this by putting "(d.s.)" after a word used with this meaning (chap. 1, sec. 3; cf. *nature (d.s.)* in chap. 2, sec. 3). Likewise, in "Screwtape Proposes a Toast" (1959)—one year before *Studies in Words*—Screwtape says:

"democracy" in the diabolical sense (*I'm as good as you,* Being like Folks, Togetherness) is the finest instrument we could possibly have for extirpating political democracies from the face of the earth. For "democracy" or the "democratic spirit" (diabolical sense) leads to a nation without great men, a nation full of cocksureness, which flattery breeds on ignorance.

Lewis does not go so far as to use an abbreviation here, but the parenthetical phrase comes close to it. A reader sees what he meant in "The Inner Ring" (1944) when he said, apropos of *The Screwtape Letters,* "The association between [the Devil] and me in the public mind has already gone quite as deep as I wish: in some quarters it has already reached the level of confusion, if not identification." Here, about fifteen years later, Lewis fuels the confusion.

The Discarded Image (1964)

During his years at Oxford, Lewis often gave two biweekly lecture courses titled "Prolegomena to Medieval Studies" and "Prolegomena to Renaissance Studies" (Gardner, 422). Lewis may have used some of his Renaissance material in his introduction to *English Literature in the Sixteenth Century.* At any rate, after giving what seems to have been a combined series at Cambridge after his professorship, he prepared the lectures for publication in 1962 (the date on the preface) as *The Discarded Image: An Introduction to Medieval and Renaissance Literature*; the book appeared in 1964, after Lewis's death.

Probably his lectures dealt with more than appears in this book, for Lewis omits such matters as the Great Chain of Being and its relationship to political hierarchy. Or perhaps (there has been no study of what his lectures included and omitted from time to time) he dropped such matters after E. M. W. Tillyard published *The Elizabethan World Picture* in 1943. No doubt in practice he referred his students to Tillyard and to Arthur O. Lovejoy's *The Great Chain of Being* (1936)—the latter gets a footnote on the Principle of Plentitude (chap. 3, sec. D).

Lewis's small book is more concerned with the reader imaginatively feeling the medieval attitude toward the Ptolemaic cosmos than with being comprehensive. It is true that Lewis spends two chapters—the third and the fourth—on the classical and late classical sources of the ideas tied to this cosmos—his most extended discussion is of Boethius's *De Consolatione Philosophiae* (chap. 4, sec. D)—but he also asks his reader two or three times to go out at night, look up at the sky, and imagine it as the medieval person did. "The facts . . . become valuable only in so far as they enable us to enter more fully into the consciousness of our ancestors. . . .

You must go out on a starry night and walk about for half an hour trying to see the sky in terms of the old cosmology" (chap. 5, sec. A). "I can hardly hope that I shall persuade the reader to yet a third experimental walk by starlight. But perhaps, without actually taking the walk, he can now improve his picture" (chap. 5, sec C; also, chap. 5, sec. B). This type of imaginative tasting—of literature or in this case of an intellectual construct—is typical of Lewis's criticism.[8]

A later chapter in the book—the seventh, "Earth and Her Inhabitants"—is often loosely tied to the book's basic discussion of the Cosmic Model. Lewis does show the relationship of the seven liberal arts to the seven "planets" (five planets, the Sun, and the Earth's Moon) (chap. 7, sec. I); but the section on medieval histories is about not the cosmos but the received past: a medieval purchaser of a historical manuscript wanted a traditional history, adjusted here and there, but basically unchanged (chap. 7, sec. H). Although he draws several analogies between the cosmos and the past, Lewis is contributing those, and he has no citations to back them up. The way the traditional past was created—from acceptance of previous authorities—is the same as the *origin* of the model, but the two results are not tied together. Another chapter—the sixth, "The *Longaevi*," about fairies mainly—is an announced escape from the rigidity of the model, and so does not fall under this objection.

Lewis is often illuminating in his contrasts between the medieval views and those of the modern period. Perhaps the highest number are in the last chapter, "The Influence of the Model," which is on the effect of established patterns on medieval literature, with contrasts with earlier and later writings. But perhaps the most surprising are two comparisons, not contrasts, with existentialism. These are surprising simply because Lewis, in most of his books, seems to have stopped keeping up with modern ideas about the time of Bergson and Shaw. Here he briefly compares a theistic existentialism (probably that of Gabriel Marcel or Martin Buber) to the *Mystical Theology* of the pseudo-Dionysius (chap. 4, sec. C); and his second, fuller comparison—to a demand by Boethius to understand why God allows so much irregularity in men's lives, as contrasted to the regularity of the heavens—involves not theistic existentialism but the more characteristic branch (probably Sartre's) (chap. 4, sec. D).[9]

In addition to the discussion of the Medieval Model mentioned above, Lewis has a polemical epilogue to his book. (If the neutral references to existentialism are evidence of the "genial" temper Helen Gardner noted in Lewis's late books, this is a touch of the old Lewis.) This epilogue is a combination of two arguments, one strong, one weak. The better part of his argument concerns the thesis that much of today's model is mathematical and cannot be pictured at all. His example is "the curvature of space," so he is probably thinking of Einstein's theories when he mentions mathematics. This has an element of truth to it, as demonstrated by the nine spatial dimensions, instead of three, hypothesized in the current "superstring" theory unifying the four elemental forces of the universe (*current* at least as these words are written).

Lewis's poorer argument is about evolution. He shows, correctly enough, that the idea of progress became popular in the century before Darwin; but he then suggests that scientists discover whatever fits the current ideas. "I do not at all mean that these new phenomena are illusionary. Nature has all sorts of phenomena in stock and can suit many different tastes." So much for geological levels of fossil remains! Lewis did a much better job of discussing evolution in "The Funeral of a Great Myth" (1967), in which he distinguished between the popular myth and the scientific hypothesis. His treatment of the myth of evolution in that essay makes a model much in the same sense he has used the word in *The Discarded Image.*

This book is obviously a literary history in a rather specialized sense. Lewis is celebrating the Medieval Model—"Few constructions of the imagination seem to me to have combined splendor, sobriety, and coherence in the same degree" (epilogue)—which is a way of allowing his readers (and, earlier, his auditors) to see, to imagine, with medieval eyes. As the model is typical of the whole period, Lewis traces no changes in it; but he does give the history of its origin and does show relationships of the literature to the model once it is developed. Lewis adds sixteenth- and seventeenth-century authors to his examples because the model was still used in poetry through that period (chap. 2), although Milton, as is well known and not mentioned here, had Raphael in *Paradise Lost* explain *both* the Ptolemaic and Copernican views of the universe.

The Discarded Image is less austerely intellectual than *Studies in Words.* The appeals to the imagination, the variety of materials, the less rigid organization, and even the mild sniping at the modern age (e.g., in chap. 5, sec. A)—all of these make for a lively book for anyone interested in the medieval period.

For the student of Lewis, this small book is almost too rich for brief discussion. Since it sums up his view of the medieval world, it also epitomizes Lewis's borrowings from that time for his writings. He refers to the three roads in "Thomas the Rymer" (chap. 6) that he used in a narrative poem "The Queen of Drum." Some brief comments on dragons (chap. 7, sec. B) sketch the background of Lewis's two poems "The Dragon Speaks" and "Dragon-Slayer," which first appeared, without titles, in *The Pilgrim's Regress*—as well as some aspects of Eustace Scrubb's adventure in *The Voyage of the "Dawn Treader"* (chaps. 6–7). The Intelligences of the seven planets (chap. 5, sec. C), the sunlight of space, and the astrology tied to the planets (both chap. 5, sec. B) were all adapted in the Ransom Trilogy. And the casual mixture of minor classical deities—nymphs, satyrs, centaurs, "tritions"—with hags, dwarfs, and giants of the Northern tradition in some of Lewis's sources in the chapter on the *Longaevi* may have encouraged his equally casual mixture in his Narnian books.

There are also more personal touches—two brief autobiographical reminiscences involving Irish fairies (chap. 6) and a comparison based on Tolkien's hobbits (chap. 8). But the intellectual side of Lewis is as significant in this book as the personal: he corrects *The Allegory of Love* on one point (chap. 8); he reuses (and comments he is reusing) the image of the cathedral as a symbol of the building process of Sir Thomas Malory's works (chap. 8)—an image that appeared at the close of his 1947 review "The *Morte Darthur*" and also at the close of his 1963 essay "The English Prose *Morte*"; he shows his movement toward an iconographic approach to medieval literature that was basic to a later book edited from his lecture notes, *Spenser's Images of Life* (chap. 4, sec D; chap. 5, secs. B, C; chap. 8). Finally, although Lewis several times points out that the Medieval Model had little to do with actual spirituality in Christianity (chap. 2; chap. 4, sec. A; chap. 5, sec. C), it is inevitable that Lewis would cite again and again Dante, for it was he who best combined—almost solely combined—the model and belief (chap. 2). Therefore, the thirty-seven page references to Dante in this book.

Chapter Four

The Generic Critic and Literary Theorist

Although literary histories seem to have held Lewis's first allegiance among his writings on literature, they are certainly not the only types of books he produced. In two of the books in this chapter, Lewis is primarily the generic critic: *A Preface to "Paradise Lost"* (1942) and *Spenser's Images of Life* (1967). In the other, he is primarily the theorist: *An Experiment in Criticism* (1961). If there had been space, two books only half by Lewis could have been added: *The Personal Heresy* (1939) and *Arthurian Torso* (1948). The former and the conclusion of the latter show Lewis the theorist also, but most of "Williams and the Arthuriad" in *Arthurian Torso* is Lewis in the role of explicator.

A Preface to "Paradise Lost" (1942)

Lewis gave a series of lectures on Milton at Oxford in 1939 and then delivered a series—presumably the first revised—as the Ballard Matthew Lectures at University College, North Wales, in 1941; the book version, with further revision, appeared the next year. In the meantime, Charles Williams had published his introduction to the World's Classics edition of Milton and had lectured on Milton at Oxford, both in 1940. Also during these years, Lewis wrote *Perelandra* (1943), his story of a Venerian Adam and Eve who did not fall. Since Lewis dedicates *A Preface to "Paradise Lost"* to Williams, citing both his lectures and the World's Classics introduction as having freed Milton from one hundred years of misunderstanding, one might expect that the book would follow the introduction closely. But the 1939 series of lectures shows that Lewis was working on his material earlier, under whatever impulse.

The first six chapters have nothing to do with Williams's introduction, and five of these, excluding the second, are the generic discussion. Genre study sounds more typical of Lewis than Williams.

Lewis defines the epic genre as Milton knew it (chap. 1); discusses what he calls the primary epic, with the *Iliad, Odyssey,* and *Beowulf* as his examples (chaps. 3–5); and, with illustrations from the *Aeneid* analyzes the secondary epic—called by others (not mentioned by Lewis) the art or imitative epic (chaps. 6–8). He suggests that the primary epic is an elevated telling of a heroic story; but, since there is no stable society in a heroic age, simply one day's victors, there is no universal theme (chap. 5). On the other hand, in Virgil's *Aeneid,* there is a theme, a national cause, a belief in enduring principles, to which a man may subordinate other desires (chap. 6).

Following the generic study, the secondary epic's style (chap. 7) is discussed in terms of Milton's emotional manipulation of his reader: the names, the allusions, the similes are used for their tonal effect, while a logical or narrative structure satisfies the mind. Lewis also discusses Milton's syntax, with a contrast to modern free verse, and ends with a long analysis, partly in Jungian terms, of Satan's approach to Paradise. The latter discussion contains a reference to a toy garden the reader made as a child—evocative of Lewis's account of his brother's toy garden in *Surprised by Joy,* which he says influenced his concept of Paradise (chap. 1).

Lewis follows his analysis of this style with a defense of it, including a defense of stock responses (chap. 8). Three aspects are of particular interest. First, in a comparison of rhetoric and poetry, Lewis says that poetry gives a concrete vision, which includes the proper emotional response, rather than being persuasive as such (rather than being mere propaganda, one might say). This is much like Lewis's theory of poetry in the fifth chapter of *The Personal Heresy.* Second, Lewis's discussion of stock responses shows that poetry does teach, if not persuade—or move to action—as rhetoric does. Since this is the Horatian and Renaissance tradition of poetry teaching by pleasing, Lewis's acceptance of it is not surprising. And Lewis's assumption about its method of teaching is much like Sir Philip Sidney's praise in *The Apology for Poetrie* of "fayning notable images of vertues, vices, or what else." Thus, one thing that Lewis believes Milton teaches (by example) is stock responses. (The Chronicles of Narnia are Lewis's clearest attempt along these lines: the moral lines are clearly, and imaginatively, drawn.) Third, the last part of the chapter is spent on the actual defense of Milton's heightened style. This, while justified in itself for Lewis's purposes, prepares for the devastating paragraph in his conclusion in which he

points to F. R. Leavis as a person who understands Milton's style
but hates it.

Up to this point, with the exception of the second chapter, Lewis
has been explaining the genre and defending the concomitant style
of Milton's poem. In chapter 9, he turns to the content. Since that
content is primarily Christian, much of what Lewis does is explain
that belief, as some of his chapter titles indicate: "Milton and St.
Augustine" (10), "The Theology of *Paradise Lost*" (12), "Satan"
(13), "The Mistake about Milton's Angels" (15), "Unfallen Sexuality" (17), "The Fall" (18). The defense of this approach, with a
reference to the criticism of Denis Saurat, appears in the ninth
chapter, "The Doctrine of the Unchanging Human Heart." Lewis
attacks the belief that human nature is always the same, although
admitting he at one time held that position—presumably when he
suggested that courtly love marked one of the few real changes in
human attitudes, in *The Allegory of Love* (chap. 1). He now believes
that, to understand the writings of other periods, one must understand what the principal concerns of those periods were: Christian
theology, in the seventeenth century. This is an implicit defense of
historical introductions; no longer is Lewis's literary history presented mainly in terms of introducing readers to what exists in the
literature of the periods—now it is explaining what the periods
themselves valued.

The reference to Saurat is typical of the Lewis of this book. Near
the end of chapter 10, Tillyard is cited as not understanding the
basic meaning of *Paradise Lost*; the eleventh chapter, "Hierarchy,"
opens with a disagreement with Dr. Johnson; the twelfth is an
extended answer to Saurat's *Milton: Man and Thinker* (1925); the
thirteenth is a reply to Blake, Shelley, and "those who admire Satan";
the fourteenth begins again against a Johnsonian position; and the
sixteenth, "Adam and Eve," opens as a reply to the statement by
Walter Raleigh (the modern critic, not the sixteenth-century gentleman). The use of Johnson's criticism as a starting place in two
instances shows that Lewis's argumentativeness is not just an anti-
modern-criticism device, but basic to his need to defend writings
and principles, to offer rehabilitations, in his essays of this period.
But the major argument in this book, that which frames it, has not
been mentioned: one with T. S. Eliot. The second chapter is a reply
to a comment by Eliot—that only good modern poets should judge
the worth of poetry—in "A Note on the Verse of John Milton"

(1936), and the last paragraph of the conclusion returns to Eliot in terms of his attitude toward Milton's poetry.

These comments on Eliot are part of what is usually called the Milton Controversy of the period. Amusingly enough, Lewis froze when Charles Williams got him together with Eliot after this book appeared and Eliot said, among other things, that he admired it. But Eliot did more than that: after reprinting his original essay as "Milton I" in *On Poetry and Poets* (1957), he included as "Milton II" a 1947 lecture in which he praises Charles Williams's introduction, mentions the twelfth chapter of Lewis's book objectively, but, more importantly, withdraws from his statement that only good poets should judge poetry, justifying both literary historians and contemporary poets from their different perspectives; he also seems to allude to Lewis's fourteenth chapter, "Satan's Followers," in his reference to critics who have shown that Moloch, Belial, and Mammon "speak according to the particular sin which each represents."

These references to Williams tie back to Lewis's book. Williams in his World Classics introduction said that Eliot's (first) essay had enlivened Miltonic criticism, indicated he agreed with some of it and disagreed with other parts, and then declined to discuss it further—but recommended it. Lewis, in his dedication, praised Williams's criticism—and then went on to apply some of it. In the thirteenth chapter, Lewis uses two of Williams's points about Satan: his sense of injured merit that leads to malice and his lies ("Hell is always inaccurate," writes Williams). Much of what Lewis suggests about Satan is original, on the other hand: the framing comparison to Sir Willough Patterne of George Meredith's *Egoist* (1879) and the tracing of the progressive degeneration of Satan, for example. Even when he borrows Williams's point about Satan's falsehoods, he expands on which lies were consciously done and which were the result of self-deception. For Satan, Lewis says, "has become more a Lie than a Liar"; it is the same distinction that George MacDonald (the character) makes about a person on the edge of damnation in *The Great Divorce*: is she a Grumbler or has she become a Grumble?

Other comments in this book are typical of Lewis. "Every poem can be considered in two ways—as what the poet has to say, and as a thing he makes" (Lewis's italics omitted). This obvious comment leads to its elaboration in the epilogue of *An Experiment in Criticism*. He immediately restates this duality in terms of the author's union of his experiences and thoughts and a preexisting genre. Since Lewis is defining the epic in this first chapter, his generic emphasis is appropriate; but two points may be made about it. First, most of his own fiction is developed in genres—science fiction, Dantean imitation, fairy tales. Second, Lewis's dismissal of originality—"It is the smaller poets who invent forms, in so far as forms are invented"—ignores the whole of romantic organicism. Walt Whitman invented his free verse form, his genre, and is a major writer, not that Lewis was likely to consider American poetry in making his statements.

Most chapters could be used this way to illustrate aspects of Lewis's other writings, or his critical biases, or his personality. Several critics have used passages from the chapters on "Adam and Eve" and "The Fall" to discuss *Perelandra,* for instance. The mention of the prohibition in the Cupid and Psyche story (chap. 10) prepares for *Till We Have Faces.* It may even be characteristic of Lewis that he uses lowest common multiple (chap. 9) when he means highest common factor. [1]

But it is also characteristic of Lewis to refer to his friends, in addition to Williams, and to Dante. Tolkien appears with an oral comment on the types of Old English poetry (chap. 3); Barfield, with a quotation from *Poetic Diction* (chap. 11). Over half a dozen references to Dante occur (at least one—in chap. 17—not in the index), the most interesting being two in which Lewis compares Milton and Dante, to Dante's advantage: Dante could have written about unfallen sexuality without Milton's failure (chap. 17), and Dante is both a better poet in artistry and a more spiritual poet than Milton (chap. 19). Also, on one side, Dante is a writer of science fiction, for the popular and the significant were not then split (chap. 15). Perhaps Lewis, like T. S. Eliot, believed in a modern "dissociation of sensibility"? This also leads to *An Experiment in Criticism.*

Dante is, however, the wrong poet with whom to leave this volume. In "Milton Read Again," a poem in *Spirits in Bondage,* Lewis calls Milton "Master." Lewis later shifted allegiances, but much of the loyalty remains. After all, the argumentation shows this is a *defense* of Milton.

An Experiment in Criticism (1961)

If a reader were to turn directly from *A Preface to "Paradise Lost"* to *An Experiment in Criticism,* one of the large differences he would find is the near absence of critics' names in the latter. A passage that discusses evaluative critics, naming ten, excludes all living critics (chap. 11). The epilogue mentions only Croce, Aristotle, and I. A. Richards—although, to be fair, Richards was also mentioned earlier (chap. 2). But there is nothing like the chapter spent disagreeing with Eliot or like the chapters begun with a named critic's view, against which Lewis argues.

This does not mean that the book is neutral in what it is saying, however. It is essentially an attack on a type of evaluative criticism— criticism that is concerned with celebrating some authors by depreciating others. Lewis's final attack is on what he calls "the Vigilant school of critics" (chap. 11); he finds them concerned with the use of literature to promote "the good life," although never defining fully their philosophy of life. In *Studies in Words* (exp. ed.), as mentioned earlier, Lewis studied F. R. Leavis's use of *life* (chap. 10, secs. 4–5, 7), once calling him a vitalist (chap. 10, sec. 8). Although Lewis's approach was there objective, there seems little reason to doubt he has Leavis and his followers in mind in this book. But he has generalized: any group that tears down the reputation of some books in order to celebrate some others on the basis of psychological benefits to the readers fits Lewis's description. This is Lewis in his Dr. Johnson mood, that of the criticism in *The Rambler,* so to speak, except that Lewis's style is always more filled with specific images than Johnson's.

Lewis's book of eleven chapters and an epilogue has a simple, if nonlinear, organization: the first four chapters establish the difference between the reading of the literary and the unliterary, with chapter three being a parallel argument from music and art; the next four chapters are clarifications of side issues ("On Myth," "The Meaning of *Fantasy,*" "On Realisms," "On the Misreadings by the Literary"); the ninth chapter summarizes the argument so far in five points, with a conclusion about pedagogy; the tenth chapter is another side issue ("Poetry"); and the eleventh chapter, "The Experiment" of the book's title, argues for the judgment of the worth of books on the basis of how they are read, concluding with the attack on the Vigilant critics. The epilogue is a statement of the value of literature.

The main argument is a deliberate advocacy of making difficult the statements of the ultimate worth or worthlessness of particular fictions. In Lewis's scheme, a critic must do surveys of how books are read: if *any* reader turns to a particular work for aesthetic pleasure,

then it cannot be damned; if *no* reader uses it for other than passing
time, excitement, or as the basis for egoistical daydreams, then it
is worthless (chap. 11). In practice, Lewis admits a critic may use
his own reaction as one piece of evidence of the aesthetic worth of
a fiction; but his reaction as to its negative worth is not valid, for
he may have a disability to appreciate certain works. This last
position suggests that what Lewis ends up arguing is this: a critic
may praise a work, but not, without elaborate evidence, attack.
Since *written* statements—as well as oral—are acceptable evidence
of a work's merits, then, although Lewis does not say so, the whole
tradition of literary praise in the past becomes testimony of the value
of certain writings.

If Lewis's main thesis proves to be an attack on artistic deval-
uation, which would (if put into effect) tend to sustain established
reputations, nevertheless two reasons to support his position are
apparent. First, it is the position of common sense. If people who
enjoy literature, either in one age or through several centuries, report
that a certain work gives them pleasure upon reading and rereading
(cf. chap. 1), then there is likely to be some merit to that work.
(The mention of rereading as a mark of literary appreciation also
appears in "On Stories" [1947].) Second, no logical reason exists to
attack one work in order to advance another: why not simply write
that the second is aesthetically well written? Likewise, there is no
reason to attack one genre in order to defend whatever pleases the
critic (chap. 11), such as attacking romances to advance realism,
one assumes. In an essay "On Science Fiction" (1966), Lewis comments that he dislikes detective stories and so he does not discuss
them.

On the other hand, this avoidance of depreciatory criticism is
unlikely to be put into practice, except by some individuals, for
three reasons, largely unmentioned by Lewis. First, since the romantic shift of *original* to be a praise term, the artist has had to
contrast himself with his predecessors in order to claim his work's
value. "Make it new!" said Ezra Pound, making a typical statement
of the antitradition tradition. Thus the artist depreciates to advance
his own works. Second, such depreciations are a magnificent way
of causing a stir. Lewis says that dethronements waste energy (chap.
11), but he underestimates the desire of people—almost all at some
times, some at almost all times—to agitate situations and cause
excitement. This is as true in literary and critical circles as any

others. Third, as Lewis mentions with his Vigilants, some writers on literature do not turn to it for aesthetic reasons but for one cause or another: they attack and defend for party concerns. Theirs is not, ultimately, a literary discussion; but it is usually confused with such discussion in its period. In contrast, as Lewis indicates, both a materialist and a Christian as critics ought to agree on the literary merits of both Lucretius and Dante (chap. 8).

The side issues in this book have been of some importance. For example, Lewis's chapter "On Myth" sometimes has been applied to Lewis's own fiction. Lewis's position is actually neither fish nor fowl—not quite what critics usually mean by psychological, by archetypal, or by mythological criticism. Lewis's myths are not universal—neither the unliterary at all nor all the literary react to them; he is only concerned with those that work at the conscious level; a myth that affects one myth-oriented reader may not affect a second. Thus, the Lewisian critic normally quotes his six characteristics of myth and then assumes the myth that the critic finds in *Perelandra,* for instance, can be appreciated, and felt, by all readers—a shift from a Lewisian to a semi-Jungian position. Lewis, when he refers to Tolkien's Ents and Lothlorien as having a mythic quality, only saves himself by stating "I should say."

Ten references to Dante occur, although the volume has no index to help with their citation. Besides the account of Lewis reading Lucretius and Dante at different ages, mentioned above, perhaps the most interesting is a statement about grief, beginning with an allusion to "The Hollow Men" by T. S. Eliot: "Real sorrow ends neither with a bang nor a whimper. Sometimes, after a spiritual journey like Dante's . . . it may rise to peace—but hardly a peace less severe than itself" (chap. 8). In the same year as this volume *A Grief Observed* appeared, which ended with a quotation from *Il Paradiso.* Since he wrote *An Experiment in Criticism* the year before it was published, Lewis may well have intended the statement about the spiritual journey to refer to, among others in its universalized form, his wife, Joy Davidman.

If references to Dante appear often in the book, an odd allusion for Lewis runs throughout, giving a structural motif to the volume. This is a series of five echoes of the last two lines of Archibald MacLeish's "Ars Poetica": "A poem should not mean / But be." MacLeish is never named, but the references are unmistakable. For example, "I am not here trying to prejudge the issue between those

who say, and those who deny, that 'a poem should not mean but
be.' Whatever is true of the poem, it is quite clear that the words
in it must mean" (chap. 4); "We have already mentioned, but not
answered, the question whether a poem 'should not mean but be' "
(chap. 8); "A work of literary art . . . both *means* and *is*. It is both
Logos (something said) and *Poiema* (something made)" (epilogue).
This is a rhetorical sequence leading to a standard, nonimagistic
position by Lewis.

For Lewis goes on to distinguish: the *Poiema* gives pleasure and,
in some sense, psychological satisfaction; the *Logos* enlarges the
reader's mental perspectives. Lewis is presenting a modified version
of the classical position: poetry (or literature) pleases and teaches.
But a mental enlargement is not the same thing as a simple didactic
emphasis.

Spenser's Images of Life (1967)

Lewis made much of his critical reputation with his long study
of *The Faerie Queene* that appeared as the last chapter of *The Allegory
of Love* in 1936. But he kept returning to Spenser. In *Studies in
Medieval and Renaissance Literature* (1966), collected after Lewis's
death, five essays on Spenser appear—perhaps one should make it
six, since "Tasso" (1966) contains an extended comparison with
Spenser. Of the five, "Genius and Genius" (1936) is *not* the same
as the appendix to *The Allegory of Love* that bears the same name,
but they cover the same material. "On Reading *The Faerie Queene*"
(1941) is a brief introduction for new readers of the poem. "Edmund
Spenser, 1552–99" (1954), written for American college students,
is interesting for its discussion of Spenser and Ireland. "Neoplaton-
ism in the Poetry of Spenser" (1961) in some points and "Spenser's
Cruel Cupid" (1966) directly forerun passages in *Spenser's Images of
Life*. In the middle of these essays comes the extended discussion
of Spenser in *English Literature in the Sixteenth Century*.

So Lewis's comments on Spenser's poems stretch from *The Allegory
of Love,* at least one per decade, to *Spenser's Images of Life*. But the
latter was not finished by Lewis: it exists as manuscript notes used
for university lectures; Alastair Fowler turned it into Lewis's final
book-length study of literature. The two manuscript pages repro-
duced in the volume indicate what Fowler's work was like, and
also—as do his occasional footnotes of disagreement—how closely
he has adhered to Lewis's content.

Lewis's general approach is far different here than it was in *The Allegory of Love*. There he began with the Italian romantic epic to establish the genre; here Boiardo is not mentioned, Ariosto appears only for a metaphor about a woman's breasts (chap. 1), and Tasso twice, in a brief catalog of epic catalogs (chap. 9, sec. 3) and in a refutation of Spenser's mention of him in "A Letter . . . to Sir Walter Raleigh" (chap. 10, sec. 2). Instead, *Spenser's Images of Life* begins with a discussion of the traditional iconography in the Renaissance, mentioning the pageant, tournament pageantry, the masque, traditional images of the gods, hieroglyphs and emblems, and philosophical iconography (introduction). A pageant was mentioned only briefly in *The Allegory of Love* (chap. 7, sec. 2). The main point is that Lewis is defining Spenser's genre in terms of iconographical imagery: Spenser writes pageants; he uses traditional imagery in his descriptions; his symbols are public, not private (introduction). Further, the characters in the story do not understand the symbols; those are for the reader (chap. 1).

In the ten chapters that follow, only the last, "The Story of Arthur," does little with such popular imagery. Lewis's first chapter begins with the golden statue of Cupid conquering a dragon seen by Britomart in the House of Busyrane. The language, he says, does not repay close reading in the New Critical sense, but the imagery— compared to other poets and to handbooks of iconography—does. Lewis compares the statue with the images of Cupid found in other poems, including Ovid's *Metamorphoses* and a song from Sidney's *Arcadia;* in an emblem book, Alciati's *Emblematum liber;* and in a painting by Botticelli. (This material is the same as "Spenser's Cruel Cupid.") One need not trace Lewis's discussion throughout to see the approach.

His emphasis on iconography means that he especially stresses the pageantlike processions and the descriptions of the "houses": for example, in the second chapter, the Temple of Venus; in the third, the Garden of Adonis; in the fourth, the Waste House motif, with the House of Orgoglio and the Cave of Mammon; in the fifth, a brief mention of Nature's witnesses in the Mutabilitie Cantos as "the greatest of all the poem's pageants"; in the sixth, the House of Coelia; in the seventh, Isis Church; in the ninth, the pageant of marine gods and rivers at the wedding of Thames and Medway.

These, and such things as the Platonic quest of Prince Arthur, discussed in the tenth chapter, are the content of the book. For a student of Lewis, however, other aspects are striking. Sometimes he is saying still what he said earlier. The famous antithesis of the Bower of Bliss and the Garden of Adonis in *The Allegory of Love* (chap. 7, sec. 3)—which caused *The Norton Anthology of English Literature* to reprint those set-pieces for years—reappears here briefly with essentially the same point (chap. 3, sec. 1).[2] On the other hand, sometimes there is change. In *The Allegory of Love,* Lewis's discussion of Isis and of Artegall under the control of Radigund (chap. 7, sec. 3) does not even mention that Britomart is the visitor to the Temple and turns to a complaint about Spenser's handling of Mercilla, who, Lewis believes, should have been used to balance Artegall's type of justice. In *Spenser's Images of Life,* however, a whole chapter (7) is titled "Britomart's Dream" (i.e., in what is now called Isis Church); Lewis argues that in the allegory Britomart is being placed as the ruler of Artegall, as Isis of Osiris and as Mercy of Justice. Also at this point the distinction between what the characters understand and what the reader sees—a distinction not made in *The Allegory of Love*—is significant; Britomart will rule Artegall, presumably by tempering his severity, but she does not know it— she looks forward to being a traditional, subordinate wife. (Lewis's treatment of Radigund—the archfeminist, so to speak—is much the same in both books, although he does not push her as a lesson for the reader in the later book.)

A few other passages are striking for reasons beyond their scholarly treatment. Lewis invents a whole passage of what may be imagined to have passed in Spenser's mind when he introduced the concept of reincarnation into the Garden of Venus (chap. 3, sec. 4): this is a good essayic device for clarity, but it is hardly scholarship. Lewis's typical combativeness in his earlier work is largely gone here; but he does wipe out a passage in a critical essay in which Derek Traversi misidentifies a Spenserian character—Diana taken to be Britomart—and reaches conclusions about Spenser's art on that basis. Lewis shows that the details of clothing, for an iconographically aware reader, should have corrected the identification and suggests that Traversi's conclusions cannot be based on his evidence (chap. 3, sec. 5). And Lewis's refutation of what Spenser said he was doing in the "Letter to Raleigh"—four passages quoted and disagreed with—is not only another argumentative passage from Lewis but a clever way rhetorically to modulate into a statement of Spenser's achievement (chap. 10, sec. 2).

Perhaps if Lewis had prepared this book for publication, more of his usual citations would have appeared. But as it is, *La Divina Commedia* is mentioned only in the first paragraph and Tolkien not at all. Charles Williams's statement of affirmative theology—"This also is Thou; neither is this Thou"—is quoted and footnoted (chap. 10, sec. 1).

And Lewis is sometimes wrong. For example, Fowler notes his disagreement with Lewis's statement that the story of Florimell is largely nonallegorical, but he gives no reason (chap. 9, sec. 2). Northrop Frye, in *Anatomy of Criticism* (138), has briefly demonstrated a nature allegory in her adventures—not a type of allegory with which Lewis concerns himself (although it would have helped his larger argument about Spenser's purpose), but certainly an allegory that makes a meaningful pattern out of both Florimell and the false Florimell.

Lewis's chapter on "Faceless Knights" (8) has been passed over until this point. Fowler in his preface speaks of "a critical new departure" in "the adumberation of a manner of approach to fiction not suitable for textual analysis." But it is not a new approach. This chapter is a new version of "On Stories" (1947), with echoed touches from the latter part of chapter 7 in *An Experiment in Criticism*. What is new is the use of Renaissance painters as evidence and a Mendelssohn letter to present an argument; but the painters, at least, are typical of the citations of Renaissance art throughout this book on Spenser. What is old is the use of evidence from fairy tales and adventure stories (Rider Haggard's *King Solomon's Mines* again the example) for forms without complex characterization, and Gulliver and Alice again as examples of appropriately simple characters placed in strange lands. The largest difference between the essay and this chapter is that "On Stories" is concerned with the moods or (in a nonintellectual sense) "ideas" of the fictions; "Faceless Knights" with the images and settings of the romances. These can be reconciled by claiming that the images create the moods. But obviously Lewis has been led to his emphasis on images here by his whole discussion of Spenser's iconography and symbolism.

A final difference is that "On Stories" saw these psychologically affecting passages as only briefly caught in the sequence of the plot, but "Faceless Knights" sees the romance (perhaps influenced by the two discussions of plots of novels in *An Experiment in Criticism*) as a sequence like a symphony in which the images, like musical motifs, are developed, modified, contrasted, half echoed. Lewis's whole discussion of how the images in *The Faerie Queene*—the various depictions of Cupid, for example—reveal their meanings in comparison prepares for this discussion. Perhaps "Faceless Knights" is better as an explanation of Spenser's poem than as a theory of all romances, but one could imagine it applied to some other works— Hawthorne's *House of Seven Gables,* for instance, where Phoebe (as a feminine version of Phoebus) "is" a sungoddess (the house is bathed in sunlight only when she is there), or Lewis's own *Till We Have Faces,* where the motif of the veil vs. bareness runs throughout.

Chapter Five
The Moral Philosopher

C. S. Lewis is not often thought of as a philosopher, but his first in Greats at Oxford in 1922 was the equivalent for an American of graduating with highest honors in philosophy—and ancient history—at the Bachelor of Arts level. Lewis's first full-time teaching position was tutoring in philosophy for a year as a replacement for a University College don who was in America as a visiting professor. It is true that Lewis wrote his father, after receiving a position in English the following year, that he was happy to give up a life dealing with abstractions, but this does not mean he abandoned all philosophic concerns.

Two of the three works to be considered in this chapter—"Right and Wrong as a Clue to the Meaning of the Universe" and *The Abolition of Man*—are in the natural-law tradition. This is a term that, outside of legal, professorial, and religious circles, may be misleading, for it does not refer to laws of nature as the phrase is used today—that is, to scientific laws. As Lewis explains in the first chapter of "Right and Wrong," it refers to a universal moral law, or a law of human nature. In the last essay Lewis wrote, "We Have No 'Right to Happiness' " (1963), he speaks of the tradition of Thomas Aquinas, Hugo Grotius, Richard Hooker, and John Locke; elsewhere, in an essay on legal morality, "The Humanitarian Theory of Punishment" (1949), he adds Aristotle and the Stoics. For Protestant Christians, the support comes from St. Paul's reference to pagans obeying the moral law by reason (Romans 2:14).

This book attempts no critique of the tradition itself, although it is fair to add that few modern secular philosophers believe in it. On the other hand, the United States was founded on it, with the assumption that certain natural rights exist. This book will be concerned only with what Lewis made of natural law.

The third book in this chapter, *The Four Loves,* is partly a religious book, but on the first page of Lewis's introduction not only is St. John quoted from the New Testament but Plato is also used as an authority. The situation becomes clearer in the chapter on friendship when Aristotle's *Ethics* and Cicero's *Amicita* are mentioned in the first paragraph (chap. 4). Lewis's book is one in the tradition of Aristotle and Cicero then; it is, of course, a Christian ethics that Lewis presents, but unlike his earlier *Christian Behaviour* (1943), discussed in the chapter on apologetics, where Lewis summed up Christian teaching, this book discusses loves that are common (except the last) to Christian and non-Christian alike, to the devout of any faith and to those of none. And while Lewis writes to Christians, much in the earlier chapters can be accepted by any reader who accepts any traditional ethics at all.

"Right and Wrong as a Clue to the Meaning of the Universe" (1942)

In August 1941 Lewis delivered a series of five radio talks over the British Broadcasting Company; the next year they were collected as a five-chapter unit, "Right and Wrong as a Clue to the Meaning of the Universe," in a small book, *Broadcast Talks* (called *The Case for Christianity* in America); finally, in 1952, Lewis revised this book and two others slightly, mainly eliminating references to World War II as in progress and spoken devices such as contractions, and published the collection as *Mere Christianity*.

Some readers may object to "Right and Wrong" being considered in this chapter on the grounds that Lewis is doing a "preparation for evangelism." This is strictly speaking quite true. Lewis's approach in his first two chapters is generally parallel to St. Pauls' in the second chapter of Romans (if the comments on the Jews not living up to the revealed Law are omitted): that is, people have consciences or an awareness of the natural law, and they do not live up to what they think they should do. Lewis at this point goes on to argue that moral law implies a mental purpose to the universe. His argument takes him as far as moral theism, and although he encourages consideration of Christianity's views in his last paragraph, he actually presents no case for the Christian religion in this series.

Thus, although Lewis is taking a first step toward a Christian argument, the fact that he approaches it through natural law and that he says little about Christianity allows this half-book to be a good starting point for seeing his philosophic position.

Lewis's opening is suitably dramatic: his first paragraph contains examples of what people say when they quarrel. He then argues that implicit in these words is an appeal to a moral code. He brings in an analogy to fouls in soccer: only if there is agreement on the rules can fouls be said to exist. So far the discussion has summed up Lewis's first two paragraphs: a dramatic opening, several vivid phrasings (not mentioned), and a comparison. The other interesting aspect of the style is the simplicity of the diction. A statistic may be helpful: in the first paragraph are 122 words, of which 84 are one-syllable words; in the second, 264 words, of which 204 are one-syllable. In one of Lewis's essays, "Before We Can Communicate" (1961), he comments on translating ideas into common language, saying that, while learned language is brief, common language takes about ten times as many words to say the same thing. Whether or not "Right and Wrong" strikes a reader as being verbose, Lewis's consciousness of what he is doing is obvious. For the original radio audience, and for a mass readership, the simplicity is a virtue.

Lewis's argument to establish natural law is an appeal to personal experience—in this case, of quarrels. He follows it up with a definition and a contrast with scientific laws. Another illustration, very effective during World War II, is that of the Germans knowing at heart the same morality as the Allies. He answers an objection—a historical denial of the same values in different cultures; in the revision in *Mere Christianity*, Lewis refers his readers to the appendix of his *Abolition of Man* for further evidence. Lewis's examples to deny cultural differences are cleverly reversed: for example, can one imagine a country where cowardice in soldiers is praised? Lewis adds other examples of the implicit nature of the moral law and then makes his second point: that no one obeys the natural law. The evidence here is an appeal to the listener's (or reader's) self-awareness; Lewis adds his own failure to obey it. There are more things that might be said about this first chapter—a joke or two, other clever analogies—but what is striking is the fact that Lewis makes only two points: people are aware of the natural law, and they do not obey it. This may reflect the above comment about common language taking many words to express ideas; certainly it shows that Lewis is taking pains to be simple and clear.

The second chapter is taken up with answering listener's objections: that the moral law is just an instinct or just the result of training. The third chapter, at first sight, seems to be a mere restatement of the first—or, rather, the part of it that gave the distinction between scientific laws and the moral law. But Lewis is actually inverting the discussion of scientific laws here. No longer is he emphasizing laws per se: here he points out that objects fall when unsupported; they do not obey a law (of gravity) qua law. But the moral law exists outside of the way people behave—because they are aware of it as separate from themselves. This step in Lewis's argument raises a number of questions about the nature of consciousness that he obviously could not deal with in his radio format of fifteen minutes—and perhaps they were not, and are not, questions that bother the mass audience.

In the fourth chapter, Lewis sets up the materialistic and theistic ("religious") views of the universe as the traditional answers to such questions as where it came from and what meaning it has. Typical of Lewis is the either/or nature of this argument. (He has an appendix to this chapter on the Life Force of George Bernard Shaw and Henri Bergson, but Lewis resolves it into the same dilemma.) On the basis of natural law perceived by man but separate from him, Lewis suggests that, from inside knowledge, so to speak, it seems likely that the basis of the universe is not materialistic but mental (and hence conscious) and moral. This, of course, is an argument by analogy: since one perceives a mental, moral order here (through one's own mentality but separated from one's own desires at times), then all the rest of the universe is likely to be of the same nature. Lewis defends the argument in several ways, but this is the essence. Indeed, Lewis uses as an illustration that of a recipient of mail: he knows what messages he is getting, and he assumes that the people in other houses are also getting like messages in the envelopes the mailman leaves them.

Lewis's argument is obviously simplistic; besides, analogies are traditionally the weakest form of proof. But, again, for a mass audience, it would work well. No one was likely to insist on separating morality from consciousness, for example (although Freud puts the superego in the unconscious area). No one was likely to advance a complete egocentric position: "No one perceives the world at all in my way." For that matter, no one was likely to say, "Why do I receive all bills and my neighbor all birthday cards?"

But, however limited by his medium this presentation of Lewis's position may be, when analyzed coolly, it *was* Lewis's personal position. His conversion was based on his reaching the same position, however more complicated his approach to it, and he is no doubt offering it partly because it was a step for him towards Christianity. These are the Landlord's Rules of *The Pilgrim's Regress* which Wisdom told John were one of the three things in the world that were not products of the world.

The Abolition of Man (1943)

While "Right and Wrong as a Clue to the Meaning of the Universe" moves to a theistic position, *The Abolition of Man,* of approximately the same date, does not. Lewis argues that natural law—here called the *Tao* (the Way), after the Chinese tradition—is a set of fundamental principles, like the axioms in geometry, which are the basis of humanity; when they are discarded, man no longer exists except as an animal, a "natural object" (chap. 3)—in Lewis's fears, an animal open for experiments.

The subtitle of the book—*Reflections on Education with Special Reference to the Teaching of English in the Upper Forms of Schools*—is misleading, since it reflects the content of only the first of the three chapters. Lewis in this first chapter begins with a school text—*The Control of Language* by Alec King and Martin Ketley, although he disguises the names—that tends to debunk objective value judgments in terms of subjective emotions. Specifically, the calling of a waterfall sublime by an observer is said by the writers to be a statement about the observer's feelings, not about the waterfall. Lewis extends this to other values: is patriotism just an emotion, without any value? A school child, taught to debunk value statements as subjective, will not find when grown any firm reason to fight in a just war, *just* being a value judgment.

Lewis argues in this chapter from this subjectivism to a denial of the Tao, by means of a tradition of certain feelings being appropriate to certain external circumstances (Coleridge, Shelley, Traherne, St. Augustine, Aristotle, and Plato are the authors cited on the point); he moves—via early Hinduism, Wordsworth, Confucius, and one of the psalms—to this being part of the natural law. That is, a child is trained in appropriate responses in order that he may, when he reaches the age of reason, perceive the ethical norms. Thus, there are two parts to a life within the Tao: reason (or conscience) to perceive it, and emotional training to act on it. The two school-text authors in their debunking destroy the emotional training that mankind needs; the chapter title, "Men without Chests," refers to people who have no appropriate responses to external circumstances.

In this first chapter, Lewis does not use a large number of metaphors—probably because his matter is sufficiently specific for his
original audience (these were the Riddell Memorial Lectures at the
University of Durham): a textbook; an illustration about a waterfall
from Coleridge; an advertisement about a cruise and Lewis's contrasting examples, the latter mentioned, not quoted; another text
with a historical writing on Australian horses and, again, brief
contrasting examples; a short illustration invented by Lewis, about
a dentist; arguments about the Tao citing authors mentioned above;
an extended example of a Roman father telling his son it is sweet
and seemly to die for his country; and a final rhetorical flourish
involving, among other images, men without chests. Obviously,
Lewis is here appealing to his audience's minds with his argument,
and he does not feel the need he had in "Right and Wrong" to
provide a series of similes and illustrations.

The second chapter, "The Way," also provides contrasts with
"Right and Wrong"—with its second chapter, as it happens. In
the earlier work, when Lewis spoke on instincts as not the same as
the moral law, he particularly used the term "Herd Instinct" that
was an obvious simplification. In *The Abolition of Man,* when he
goes through basically the same arguments, he speaks of "the preservation of the species" and of "sexual desire" as instincts. But since
his arguments are essentially general, applying to any instincts, he
does not try to list the instincts or to present arguments about
specific ones, except for the claim of the quasi-evolutionary "preservation of the species."

The rest of this second chapter provides Lewis's basic argument
for the Tao. First, he analyzes the moral assumptions of the main
textbook he is studying, finding it to be—in a rather devastating
manner—those of its authors' period between the World Wars.
Second, he shows that its approach provides no means of moving
from "this is good" to "this ought to be done." His example is in
terms of preservation of society and a soldier dying for his country.
Although Lewis says he is picking this example only because it
clarifies issues (as it does), he also chooses an example that in 1943—
when Britain was fighting Nazi Germany—was emotionally loaded
for his audience. Third, Lewis sets up the Tao as moral axioms or
premises, and argues that innovators in morals are taking one or
two parts of the Tao as basic and using them against the rest—
without being able to validate their own choices if the other parts

are invalid. Lewis perhaps has in mind such an individual as George
Bernard Shaw (in Shaw's later phases) in his description of those
innovators who put feeding and clothing poor people first, ignoring
justice and good faith, for this may reflect the Shavian combination
of socialism and rule by the superman. Or it may be meant to
suggest the prewar Mussolini. But in this and Lewis's other example
of the extreme nationalist (Hitler is a possible example), Lewis names
no names. He has been depreciated occasionally, and particularly
in *An Experiment in Criticism,* as setting up straw men to attack in
his books. But Lewis, an admirer of Dr. Johnson, seems to be writing
in the eighteenth-century fashion of generalized descriptions that
could therefore be eternally valid. The supplying of some names
above (and in the discussion of *An Experiment in Criticism* elsewhere)
shows the reader's approach in validating Lewis's arguments.

Lewis makes further points in the second chapter, particularly
concerning progress within the Tao, but the above are the main
ones for his attack on current moral assumptions. In the third
chapter, "The Abolition of Man," Lewis treats of the possibility of
reshaping mankind by scientific methods so that subsequent men
can no longer perceive the Tao, but are programmed for chosen
imperatives. He states this two ways, of which the first is remi-
niscent—without mentioning the book—of the crèches in Aldous
Huxley's *Brave New World.* The ideas in this chapter are the basis
for Lewis's science-fictional presentation of the National Institute
of Co-ordinated Experiments in *That Hideous Strength.* Lewis's fears
of control by the state (meaning certain individuals in the state)
were a strong element in his personality. For example, Lewis worried
about the attempts of prisons to reform prisoners, instead of punish
them, for it implied that an individual warden had the power to
decide when a prisoner had changed ("The Humanitarian Theory
of Punishment"). Obviously today, with the growing scientific
knowledge of basic genetics, the dangers for controlled breeding of
types of men is closer than it was when Lewis wrote; his concern is
not wholly theoretical.

The Four Loves (1960)

To turn from Lewis's emphasis on natural law in the 1940s to
his discussion of love in 1960 is to turn from a theory of meaning
to an attempt to understand life as it is lived; from the basis of

ethics to their practice. If there is a pattern to *The Four Loves*, it is
that Lewis sets up one type of love after another, makes distinctions
about the varieties each takes, and praises some and points to the
dangers of others. He is neither a foolish enthusiast nor a whole-
hearted debunker. The result is that a reader sees complexity where
before (probably) he or she had not.

Lewis begins the first chapter with a distinction between Need-
love and Gift-love, and then points out his problems with the
distinction. In the second chapter, "Likings and Loves for the Sub-
human," Lewis finds Need-pleasures and Pleasures of Appreciation,
and the comparison of these with the original duality produces
Appreciative Love. And so it goes, with Lewis using these terms—
Need-love, Gift-love, Appreciative Love—as necessary, until he
reaches the last chapter, "Charity," in which these distinctions multiply like jack-rabbits in Australia: God's Gift-love, God having no
needs; humanity's natural Need-loves and Gift-loves; Divine Gift-
love given to mankind and supernatural Need-loves of God and of
each other also given by God; supernatural Appreciative Love of
God. These various distinctions in the last chapter do not necessarily
create a flaw in that part, but they do suggest a different, more
analytic, tone to Lewis's discussion there.

The second chapter is highly interesting for Lewis's treatment of
two of the "not personal" loves. The second is the love of a person's
country, in which the dangers and some of the distinctions are well
known. Lewis finds five different elements in patriotism, some of
which he is able to illustrate from Chesterton and Kipling. (One
of the pleasant things about this late book is how Lewis's knowledge
of literature has found a secondary function as illustrative of life.)
But more valuable—at least to students of the romantics—is his
treatment of the British and Russian love of nature. Lewis discusses
the dangers of going to nature to find morals, as in Wordsworth.
Nature gives images whether of peace, sublimity, beauty, gaiety,
struggle, sexual desire, or decay. "The only imperative that nature
utters is, 'Look. Listen. Attend.' " This emphasis on attending to
the object is part of Lewis's discussion in *An Experiment in Criticism*
of how one should approach the various arts. It was typical of Lewis
in meeting people, as well as in his own reading: the first thing to
do is to surrender to the experience; later, if necessary, one can
judge. Perhaps it was developed in Lewis as he, in his role of tutor,
listened to his students' papers.

The third chapter, "Affection," follows the pattern briefly established above: the term is defined and illustrated, combined with other loves, given an odd characteristic of being not primarily an Appreciative Love, distinguished from its usual praise in certain dangers of its Need and Gift characteristics, and discussed in terms of man's fallen nature. The use of examples in the extended passage on Affection's dangers is well handled: Mr. Pontifex from *The Way of All Flesh* and King Lear from Shakespeare's play, both showing the demand for Affection from children; an anecdote from *Tristram Shandy* to show good domestic manners; Mrs. Fidget, an invented character in the eighteenth-century essay style, who demonstrates the misuse of Affection as a Gift-love—Lewis has an epitaph (no. 10 in *Poems*) that makes the same point as the conclusion of this example; and Dr. Quartz, another invented character, who cannot enjoy his students becoming independent of his guidance. Although Mrs. Fidget is in the eighteenth-century style, Goldsmith's essays are a better example than Johnson's: she is a type character, but she is particularly developed. Perhaps it should be added that the treatment of *King Lear is* reductionistic qua literature; Lewis is not discussing the play but pointing a moral.

The essay on friendship (chap. 4) is, as has been noted, in the classical tradition. But if anyone compares it to the treatment of friendship in Aristotle's *Nicomachean Ethics,* he or she will find great differences. Aristotle spends much space discussing whether or not one friend can get back equivalent gifts to those that he gives. The whole business—*business* almost literally—seems mercantile, although it is based on equivalencies, not on profit. Of course, there are passages in Aristotle that rise above this, but much of the material simply seems alien to the modern understanding of friendship. (It is much more like some modern party-giving calculations: "Whom do we owe? If we invite So-and-so, will he invite us to the next one of those fashionable bashes he throws?")

Lewis sets up Companionship as the matrix of Friendship: among those who get together for some reason—hunting, drinking, studying, painting, praying—there may be two or three who see some special aspect of the truth, and so are drawn into closer relationship. Lewis, of course, sees the dangers of friendship—that the mutual interest that brings the friends together may be an illegal or a sinful one and that pride may rise out of the "we three or four" nature of friendship.

There are many other aspects of this chapter that could be discussed; but most of these topics are passed over in favor of one—the chapter's autobiographical nature. This passage appears:

In each of my friends there is something which only some other friend can fully bring out. . . . Now that Charles is dead, I shall never again see Ronald's reaction to a specifically Caroline joke. Far from having more of Ronald, having him "to myself" now that Charles is away, I have less of Ronald.

The names obviously refer to Charles Williams and J. Ronald R. Tolkien. Humphrey Carpenter, in *The Inklings,* refers to this chapter as a guide to understanding that group (167–68). Unfortunately, Carpenter's chapter on the basis of the Inklings proceeds to eliminate all of the things that the group had in common—because they differed on them in degree—until he is left with nothing but Lewis's gift for friendship (171). Lewis, however, says here that, in becoming friends, agreeing about the answer to a question is not as significant as agreeing about the importance of the question. The fact that Lewis, Williams, and Tolkien all agreed, for example, about the truth of Christianity and the importance of literature is more significant than that their Christian beliefs had different emphases and their literary tastes did not wholly coincide.

Lewis describes this chapter as a "rehabilitation," echoing the title of his first collection, *Rehabilitations and Other Essays* (1939), in which he tried to return Shelley and William Morris to favor; here he is attempting to restore friendship to the modern world—a world that calls mere acquaintances friends; but Lewis knew what he was writing about. Oddly, but perhaps revealing something of his own consistency, Lewis never mentions the ending of a friendship in his chapter.

Lewis had also experienced—in his marriage to Joy Davidman—the "being in love" that he calls Eros and the sexuality he calls Venus, before he wrote the next chapter. But, although Lewis comments about some of his ignorance of the nature of Eros when he wrote *The Allegory of Love,* the chapter does not have the same sort of autobiographical emphasis as the previous. The organization may be said to be typical in that extended definitions are followed by a discussion of the modern dangers of taking Venus too seriously and of the modern beliefs that Eros (by itself) leads to happiness and is an appropriate "Law" to follow. Perhaps because his marriage was such a short one—four years from the registry office marriage to Joy Davidman's death—and the sexual element in it shorter still, due to his wife's cancer of the bones, Lewis submits his comments for corrections by others; but since Lewis is taking stands against many modern positions—the seriousness of sex, the celebration of the body, the naked person as the true person, Shavian evolution via sexual attraction, being in love as an excuse for many sins—the humility is also good rhetoric. This chapter is more argumentative and less exemplary than the others, but Lewis often illuminates ideas with concrete images and with wit: "He [the husband married to a flawed wife] is a King Cophetua who after twenty years still hopes that the beggar-girl will one day learn to speak the truth and wash behind her ears." Feminists will not care for Lewis's one-sided discussion of the flawed wife in this passage—what husband is without flaws?—but compared to his earlier discussion of the headship of the husband in *Christian Behaviour* (chap. 6), this at least emphasizes love and service, not rule; perhaps it was marriage to a physically flawed wife that had taught Lewis this.

And now the sixth and last chapter, "Charity." The emphasis on types of loves—natural and supernatural Need-loves, Gift-loves, and Appreciative loves—has been mentioned above. This chapter, having no warning about the limits of Charity, has more analysis. Perhaps a just analogy is to the effect of Dante's *Paradiso* on the usual reader of his *Inferno* and *Purgatorio*: much more austere. Not that the chapter begins this way: the extended comparison of natural loves to a garden, besides summing up the limits of Affection, Friendship, and Eros, is a pleasant opening.

For a student of Lewis, another brief analogy—"Anodos has got rid of his shadow," in reference to a man who has given up claiming his own merits—is equally delightful. Lewis refers to his "master, [George] MacDonald," at the first of the book; here is an allusion to *Phantastes,* the small volume that, read in 1916, began the baptism of Lewis's imagination. Three years before his death, Lewis is still referring to it. (What the average reader, who certainly has not read MacDonald, will make of it, is a different question: perhaps that is why the allusion is brief.)

In his argument for the raising of natural loves to the supernatural level, Lewis uses a phrase from the Athanasian Creed: "Not by conversion of the Godhead into flesh, but by taking of the Manhood

into God." Obviously, as was stated earlier, this chapter will not
be acceptable to non-Christians, who (in this instance) do not acknowledge the validity of the Creed. But this particular phrase is
of interest: Lewis's attention may have been drawn to it by Charles
Williams who tended to cite it. In "Sexuality and Substance" (1939),
a discussion of D. H. Lawrence, Williams uses the Athanasian phrase
to indicate the truth that Lawrence missed; in a novel *War in Heaven*
(1930), Williams has an archdeacon meditate on the phrase in connection with the conversation of another clergyman whose talk tends
to work in the other direction, making heavenly things earthly.
Lewis uses the Athanasian phrase elsewhere: for example, in "Transposition" (1949)—a sermon preached in 1944—Lewis begins with
the question of what is hysteria in the phenomenon called "speaking
in tongues" and what is spiritual message; he concludes by applying
his answer to the Incarnation (the second of his four points at the
end), with the use of this creedal phrase. No doubt some other
motif could be traced through the Inklings, or some of them, just
as easily; but this use of a phrase from the Athanasian Creed does
suggest a communality of interests.

The Four Loves, excepting this specialized last chapter, shows a
knowledge of human love, its varieties, significances, and dangers.
It is a partial *Ethics,* but an essential part.

Chapter Six
The Apologist

Lewis was a Christian apologist in the Latin root meaning of *apologia*: a defender. His training in argumentation under Kirkpatrick had prepared him to argue for his positions. After his return to Christianity in 1931, his turn to logical defenses of that faith is not surprising. Beyond the three books considered below—*The Problem of Pain,* most of *Mere Christianity,* and *Miracles*—in 1942 Lewis accepted the presidency of the Socratic Society at Oxford, which included the "discussion" of the arguments of anti- and non-Christian speakers.

Austin Farrer, in his essay "The Christian Apologist," makes a distinction between an apologest per se, who answers opponents, and an advocate, who advances arguments for a position—in this case, the Christian faith (Gibb, 23). Lewis is both, of course; but much of his writing of this period begins from a defensive position. Even the oddest chapter in *The Problem of Pain,* that on "Animal Pain," begins by saying the suffering of animals is worth discussing because "whatever furnishes plausible grounds for questioning the goodness of God is very important indeed." That is, the topic must be examined because someone might (or, perhaps, someone has) used it to deny an aspect of Christianity. This is a very generalized opponent, but the argumentative position *is* a defensive one. (One remembers how often the chapters in the latter part of *A Preface to "Paradise Lost,"* two years later, begin from specific critics; despite the difference in concreteness, the rhetorical position is the same.)

Some of Lewis's essays deal with apologetics or advocacy, rather than just *being* them. The best of these is "Christian Apologetics" (1945) in which Lewis mentions a number of things he has learned from his military audiences—words that do not mean what educated speakers mean by them, and the lack of a sense of sin in the modern world, for example. Lewis also comments that he does not have the ability to give an emotional appeal, but has seen it done effectively by others.

In the last paragraph, Lewis comments that defending articles of faith is dangerous to one's own faith—because, for the moment, the defense "has seemed to rest on oneself" solely, which is a position of pride. He says much the same thing, more thoroughly, in a poem, "The Apologist's Evening Prayer" (1964).

A final point: since these books are apologetics, rather than scholarly or imaginative works, the references to Dante are sparse. In *The Problem of Pain,* one brief reference, listed in the index, and an allusion back to the first passage, not in the index. In *Mere Christianity,* probably due to its aim at a mass audience, no references. In *Miracles,* one minor reference; the index notes two, but it is wrong about the second.

The Problem of Pain (1940)

Lewis was invited to write a book on pain in the Christian Challenge series by a publisher impressed with *The Pilgrim's Regress.* Lewis's volume—or at least individual chapters—was read to the Inklings, and the book is dedicated to them. Dr. R. E. Havard, one of the group, contributes a brief appendix on his observations on patients' reactions to pain. (Charles Williams's *The Forgiveness of Sins* [1942], in the same series, is also dedicated to the Inklings.)

Lewis's book consists of ten chapters, of which the two beginning the second half, the sixth and seventh, are titled "Human Pain" and "Human Pain, *continued*" and sum up his main topic. But Lewis begins, "Introductory," by establishing the background for the intellectual problem: he shows that Christians and other moral theists do not argue from the universe to God, but rather find God in two ways, the experience of the numinous and intellectual apprehension of the moral law, which are then often identified as to source. (Christians add to their belief the Incarnation of God.) Rhetorically, Lewis's opening is arresting—"when I was an atheist"—and it gives substance to his denial of the argument from undesign. Some of Lewis's antitheistic lyrics in *Spirits in Bondage* show that that argument at one time had been meaningful to him.

It is tempting to see this argument from the numinous to be parallel to Lewis's personal accounts of *Sehnsucht,* just as the emphasis on natural law obviously ties to Lewis's intellectual reasons for conversion to theism. It *may* be, but Lewis here begins from Rudolf Otto's *The Idea of the Holy* (in German, 1917), which assumes that a feeling of awe in the presence of the Wholly Other lies at the core of all religions. This sounds far stronger than the romantic longings that Lewis describes for himself. Certainly, he does not make the claim.

Lewis does not insist that the thesis of the numinous, antithesis of the moral, and synthesis of moral theism is a necessary dialectical development, but only one that the Jews in their religion generally and other great teachers individually have made. Lewis's argument for adding the Incarnation to moral theism is, as usual in his popular apologetics, brief and simplistic. Here he says that, given Jesus's claims for himself, he was either divine (as he said) or a madman. This argument probably goes back to John 10:19–21:

> There was . . . a division among the Jews because of these words. Many of them said, "He [Jesus] has a demon, and he is mad; why listen to him?" Others said, "These are not the sayings of one who has a demon." (RSV)

Indeed, when Lewis restates the argument in *Mere Christianity,* he sets up a three-fold dilemma, making a distinction between two terms that the Jews in the quotation do not: either Jesus is divine or he is "a lunatic—on the level with the man who says he's a poached egg—or else [he is] the Devil of Hell" (bk. 2, chap. 3). One remembers that in *Surprised by Joy* Lewis tells of his arguing himself into moral theism but being converted less rationally to Christian belief. Probably he feels that the step from theism to Christian faith is not as presentable in his sort of intellectual terms as the first, and that his main work (explicit in *Mere Christianity*) is to keep a reader from saying Jesus is a great human moral teacher.

It is only when a powerful, moral God is posited that there is a problem of pain in the universe: why, Lewis asks in his second chapter, does the Christian God allow it? He begins with an elaborate syllogism, the major premise consisting of two related conditional statements; the minor premise denying the conclusion of the first conditional statement (and implicitly that of the second statement); and the conclusion therefore denying the first part of either or both the beginning conditions. If God is good, he will want his creature happy; if He is omnipotent, he can do whatever he wants. But humans—his creatures—are not happy. Therefore . . . . Lewis goes on to question the popular meanings of the words as used in the syllogism—"Divine Omnipotence" in the second chapter, "Divine Goodness" and true human happiness in the third; in short, to deny the validity of the major premise.

The next two chapters, "Human Wickedness" and "The Fall of Man," open with a statement much like one point in the essay "Christian Apologetics": until modern people realize they are sinful, Christianity has little to say to them. The first of these two chapters attempts to convince the readers of their sinfulness, and the second is a fascinating attempt to establish the doctrine of Original Sin without being literalistic about Adam and Eve. Lewis offers "a 'myth' in the Socratic sense, a not unlikely tale." The myth (or fabulous history) starts with the evolution of mankind as animals to which, at some point in time, God gave the gift of self-consciousness and awareness of the true, the good, and the beautiful— Lewis does not point out the Platonism in the triple awareness. The rest of the account covers the Fall—that is, an act of self-will— and then dwindles into reflections on the event. This is not as concrete or specific as a Socratic myth often is, but the reader of Lewis can turn to the end of the ninth chapter of *The Magician's Nephew* to see Aslan breathing on animals and thus making them talking beasts to see the first part of this account vitalized. What is significant in *The Problem of Pain* is that Lewis does not believe the Adam and Eve story can be taken seriously by his audience at a literal level in a Darwinian age.

The first of the two chapters on "Human Pain" is the more significant one. A few personal touches appear: a brief discussion of sadism as an exaggeration (and hence perversion) of normal love, referring to it as among "the ugliest things in human nature," reminds a reader of Lewis's sadistic daydreams in his teenage letters to Arthur Greeves—Lewis is impersonally denouncing what he once enjoyed; a brief anecdote about his brother and him in their childhood days is a rare foreshadowing of Lewis's accounts of their drawings in *Surprised by Joy*. But Lewis's thesis is that pain awakens mankind to its human limits; he twice uses the image of pain as God's megaphone. Pain keeps mankind from accepting this world as a be-all; it may, but it need not, lead people to believe in God. Austin Farrer, in his excellent essay on this book, comments that Lewis sees the moral half of the truth, but that pain is also "the sting of death, the foretaste and ultimately the experience of sheer destruction" (Gibb, 40).

The chapters on "Hell" and "Animal Pain" are on special aspects of pain—the eternal suffering of the damned, and the suffering of animals in their carnivorous hierarchy. Perhaps four points from these chapters show Lewis's ideas that he displays elsewhere. First, in "Hell," he comments that second and later chances at salvation may be given dead souls, but only if God in his omniscience sees possibilities (certainties?) of salvation. Perhaps this is only a strategic allowance in the argument here, but in *The Great Divorce,* five years later, Lewis shows souls getting another chance—however, most of them are not saved. Second, in "Animal Pain," Lewis has a passage depreciating acceptance of climates of opinion; this is the reversal of his early, pre-Christian chronological snobbery for the present— and Barfield, he says in *Surprised by Joy,* was responsible for his abandonment of it (chap. 13). Third, Lewis's conjecture that the higher animals may gain immortality through their masters—while it drew a letter of objection from Evelyn Underhill, in favor of wild animals—explains the animals who surround Sarah Smith, the saint of *The Great Divorce.* Finally, Lewis's conjectures about some animals' corporate selves may explain why he was so impressed by the first Charles Williams book he read, *The Place of the Lion,* four years before this book. Alternately, the archetypal animals of Williams, including the titular lion, may lead to Lewis's reference to "Lion-hood" and "a rudimentary Leonine self" here.

The final chapter, "Heaven," is generally unlike the other chapters in tone. It begins with a description of the emotional appeal of *Sehnsucht* that draws individuals toward Heaven; here Lewis assumes that all people have "these immortal longings." This and "The Weight of Glory," the year after this book, are Lewis's most important statements about *Sehnsucht* between *The Pilgrim's Regress* and *Surprised by Joy,* despite not having their framing works' personal application. Some of Lewis's statements in the middle of the chapter, such as that about the saints being all different since for each the longing has been somewhat different or that about the self-abdication of the saved, are perhaps closer to the previous tone of argument. The emphasis on self-abnegation here explains Owen Barfield's difficulties with the Christian Lewis who seemed to deliberately suppress self-knowledge: Lewis was trying to live by the principles he announced.

Just before the liturgical close of the chapter, Lewis introduces the image of the dance. This image in a limited way ties the book together. In the fifth chapter, Lewis described the universe ("world")

as a dance "in which good, descending from God, is disturbed by
evil, arising from the creatures." Lewis is here correcting the exaggeration of the implications of God's foreknowledge of the Fall,
but the image is important. In the next chapter, in a very brief
image, the act of doing good, of obeying God's commandments to
do good, is called the "tread[ing] of Adam's dance backward"—in
short, learning to obey instead of rebel. At the end of the book,
these touches are developed in a seven-sentence image of Heaven as
a dance. It is not that the image is used in the same way each of
the three times; it is just that a motif is introduced, reintroduced,
and then used in some detail. Consciously or accidentally, the celebration in the last chapter has been prepared for. (The best known
example of this image in earlier English literature is Sir John Davies's
Orchestra, a Poem of Dancing [1596], mentioned in *English Literature
in the Sixteenth Century;* Lewis elaborates the image as the Great
Dance at the end of *Perelandra,* published three years after *The Problem
of Pain.*)

Mere Christianity (1942–44; rev. 1952)

Due to the publication of *The Problem of Pain,* Lewis was invited
to give a series of religious radio broadcasts over the B.B.C. His
first series, "Right and Wrong," has been discussed in the previous
chapter. The second series, "What Christians Believe," was given
in 1942. As stated before, these two series were printed together.
The third series, "Christian Behaviour," was broadcast in 1942 and
published in an expanded form in 1943. The fourth series, "Beyond
Personality: The Christian View of God," was broadcast in 1944
and published later that year. In 1952 Lewis's revised version of
these four series appeared as *Mere Christianity.* Very occasionally,
his correcting eye missed a reference, as when an "I said last week"
appears (bk. 3, chap. 12).

The general movement of these four series of addresses—called
books in *Mere Christianity*—is clear. Book 1 argues for moral theism.
Book 2 moves through a variety of religious beliefs to Christianity
and offers a brief account of the Atonement and the bases for Chris-
tian life. Book 3 (to be considered more thoroughly below) is on
Christian morality. And book 4 had a different subtitle for broadcast:
"Beyond Personality: or First Steps in the Doctrine of the Trinity."
It took up these two parts in reverse order: the first four chapters,

approximately, consider the Trinity, and the last seven, the individual Christian's need to die to his natural personality and to accept spiritual life from Christ in its place, to go "beyond personality." In short, the volume moves through a preparation for Christian faith, an argument for it, a Christian ethics, and, Lewis suggests (bk. 4, chap. 8), the main—the only significant—further step in the Christian life.

The structure of "Christian Behaviour" can be taken as an example of the smaller-scale structure and can also be discussed in terms of what it reveals about Lewis's approach to his material. When it was first published as a separate work, Lewis indicated on the contents page which chapters were approximately as they were given on the air and which were added for book publication. With the chapter numbers from *Mere Christianity*, the original talks were these:

1. The Three Parts of Morality
3. Social Morality
4. Morality and Psychoanalysis
5. Sexual Morality
7. Forgiveness
8. The Great Sin
11. Faith
12. Faith

In the first chapter, Lewis divides morality into personal, dealing with the inner self; social, dealing with relationships between individuals; and goalistic, dealing with the overall purposes of the adjustments undertaken in the first two. Since Lewis has made his arguments for Christianity in his previous book, "What Christians Believe," the overall purposes are simply assumed to be Christian in the rest of this book. Lewis uses an extended analogy of ships at sea—both a British and a wartime interest—to support his division: the ships must run internally, must not interfere with each other, and must have a port of destination.

The next chapters develop one side of this opening. "Social Morality," as its title indicates, mainly is concerned with society, not the individual. Christianity, Lewis suggests, supplies the principles—such as the Golden Rule—but not the applications for different times and cultures. He then offers three comments on the Christian society: (a) the New Testament suggests one that is leftist in economics and rightist in family hierarchy and manners; (b) the ancient Greeks and Hebrews and the medieval Christians all denounced the loaning of money at interest; (c) the giving to the poor is an essential part of Christian morality. With this Lewis's comments on society are finished, and he turns to the individual.

"Morality and Psychology" eliminates Freudian and other psychoanalytic help as a competitor to Christian morality. In private life, Lewis was hostile to Freudianism (LCSL, 179), but here he quietly distinguishes between Freud's philosophy, which is antireligious, and his psychoanalysis, which helps a person reach a point at which he can make moral choices—at that point, Christian (or some other) morality becomes pertinent. Then Lewis alternates between discussions of evil and good: "Sexual Morality" (the corruption of the modern world, with a delightful analogy of a country in which food is gradually revealed striptease fashion); "Forgiveness" (opened in terms of forgiving the Gestapo, which in 1942 was attention catching); "The Great Sin" (pride); and two aspects of "Faith" (belief as a virtue, trust in God).

When Lewis revised these talks for publication, he added these chapters:

    2. The "Cardinal Virtues"
    6. Christian Marriage
    9. Charity
    10. Hope

Three of these chapters are interesting because they show Lewis the traditionalist in a special way. In the second chapter he begins a discussion of the seven virtues with the four that belong to the general human morality: Prudence, Temperance, Justice, and Fortitude. Then he adds Charity (chap. 9) and Hope (chap. 10) to Faith (chaps. 11–12)—the three theological virtues—to round out a discussion of all seven. Obviously, the three parts of morality (chap. 1) were not, for obscure reasons, satisfactory; he felt a need to add the number and division (4 + 3) of virtues as commonly given in the Middle Ages. The combining of both bases and resulting sequences in one book gives a greater complexity or a poorer organization (or both), as a critic wishes to argue.

"Hope" is of particular interest as another statement by Lewis of his *Sehnsucht* theme. It is here generalized: not put in terms of nature and books, as Lewis experienced it, but in terms of desire for various things—love, foreign travel, learning. Lewis says that, for the Christian, this yearning—never completely satisfied in this world—is meant to arouse a desire for Heaven, the "Hope" of the chapter title.

The chapter of Christian marriage supplements that on sexual morality; in it Lewis argues for the permanence of Christian marriage (not the same as secular marriage) and for masculine headship of the family. Logically, Lewis should have argued just for masculine headship of the Christian, not necessarily the secular, marriage; but, while beginning that way, he seems to drift into a general statement. Obviously, it is chapters such as this that have endeared Lewis to conservative readers. But this is unfair. By the time Lewis wrote *The Four Loves*, about seventeen years later (and as discussed in the last chapter), Lewis was still biblical but he was emphasizing the second half of St. Paul's phrase (Ephesians 5:25), stressing the husband's self-sacrifice. It is still not a position to delight any feminist, but it is also not one to give great comfort to the typical male supremist.

The other two books may be treated more briefly, since their theses were given above. An interesting image that runs throughout "What Christians Believe," no doubt especially effective in World War II when Germany was occupying much of Europe and wanting to invade England, is that of the world as enemy-occupied territory—that is, controlled by Satan. Lewis complicates this by having the rightful king landed in disguise to lead a sabotage campaign— that is, Christ is incarnated to overthrow Satan's rule. "Landed" suggests an invasion from sea, which was not unusual for saboteurs in Europe during that war. This image first appears at the end of the second chapter, is repeated at the opening of the fourth, and reappears in terms of God's invasion (Judgment Day) at the end of the fifth. The close of this book with the latter passage shifts from the usual clear exposition of these radio addresses to a more urgent appeal to make a Christian decision. Lewis uses three rhetorical questions in the last paragraph; four *when* clauses in four consecutive sentences; three *something*'s in one sentence; three *it will be* and one *that will not be* in four sentences; and, in four sentences, *choose, choose, choosing, chosen, choose.*

"Beyond Personality" may be used to mention one of Lewis's personal themes—perhaps paradoxically, given its title. But the same point that was made in the discussion of *The Problem of Pain* can be made here. Lewis's emphasis on dying to a person's own personality, accepting Christ's personality—pretending to be Christ until one becomes a son of God (bk. 4, chap. 7)—is the probable cause of the statement by Owen Barfield that he felt as if he saw two Lewises in the same body after his conversion: Lewis was attempting to suppress his old self, the Old Adam in Christian terms.

In general, *Mere Christianity* fulfills Lewis's statement in his essay "Before We Can Communicate" that it takes ten times as many words to say something in popular speech as it does in a learned vocabulary. Lewis, in these radio addresses, explains matters simply and uses an analogy for every difficult idea. This makes for a delightful book to introduce a person without a theological background to Christianity; the book is worth reading for a minister or other theologically educated person for the freshness of the analogies and the clarity of the ideas; but the wordiness will damage the book's rereadability for someone whose main concern is artistry. In short, Lewis wrote very well for his evangelical purposes, but simplified radio addresses do not make for the greatest nonfiction prose. Better one page of *Walden* (so far as style is concerned) than ten of *Mere Christianity*.

Miracles (1947, rev. 1960)

The third of Lewis's apologetic works has a subtitle: *A Preliminary Study*. This is important, for Lewis is producing an argument that miracles are possible—as outside, supernatural interferences to nature—not that they are common or that any particular, non-New Testament ones really happened. Lewis prefaces the book with a 1946 poem of his, untitled here but called "The Meteorite" in *Poems*, in which a meteor, having fallen from the heavens, is worked on by Earth's weather and moss as what is left of it becomes part of Earth's process. It is a clear analogy: a miracle also comes from elsewhere (Heaven, rather than outer space), and, once the supernatural moment is over, whatever has been changed becomes part of the natural processes of the universe.

Most of the controversy about this book has arisen over Lewis's argument in the third chapter (part of a longer discussion, running from the second through the sixth chapter) that a naturalist—that is, one who believes that the naturalistic cause-and-effect chain controls all of life and the universe—cannot defend reason as leading to rational conclusions. Obviously, he believes that the mind and all of its thoughts are the products of causes that did not originate in reason; therefore, he is arguing that irrationality produces rationality. Further, he contradicts himself by assuming that he can use his reason to argue for the universe being controlled by cause and effect.

Is Lewis arguing with a legitimate point of view in this chapter? Yes. Sigmund Freud is one example. Freud, in order to make psychoanalysis "scientific," argued that *all* thoughts and dreams had causes that, at least in theory, could be found. Likewise, B. F. Skinner has assumed this point of view, denying free will, in his behaviorism. Naturalism, as Lewis uses the term, is a widely assumed, if often unexamined, position on the fringes of science: a scientific, cause-and-effect fatalism.

But the controversy over Lewis's third chapter, "The Self-Contradiction of the Naturalist," came from G. E. M. Anscombe, a woman, a Roman Catholic, and a philosopher. On 2 February 1948 she read her "Reply to Mr. C. S. Lewis's Argument that 'Naturalism' Is Self-refuting" to the Socratic Club, and she and Lewis debated the topic afterwards. The primary materials and the significant secondary items can be traced through the notes in Peter J. Schakel's *Reason and Imagination in C. S. Lewis.*[1] Schakel lists Lewis's defeat by Anscombe as one of the four factors that caused him to turn from apologetics. Certainly Lewis revised that third chapter of *Miracles* in the 1960 edition, retitling the chapter "The Cardinal Difficulty of Naturalism."

The longer, second version of the chapter argues not from the previous thesis but from two senses of *because*: the Cause and Effect relationship, and the Ground and Consequent relationship. Lewis says that the former is the basis of science (this produces that) while the latter is the only method of validation of truth (from this is inferred, or on this is based, that). And the two systems cannot be reconciled.

What is certainly true is that the revised version of the chapter is more difficult and less readable as an essay than the first version. Anscombe has driven Lewis to be more rigorous, to the diminution of his ability to communicate. It is a pity that he did not write his revised argument as a third appendix to the book and put a footnote in the original chapter warning the reader about the two senses of

because and referring him or her to the back of the volume; or that
he did not expand his book by a chapter or two if that was necessary
to combine rigor and readability. As it is, precision of thought has
led to loss of literary merit.

This is an assertion, not a proof. But a reader of the seventh and
subsequent paragraphs of the original and the revised chapters—
this being their point of variation—will find two paragraphs in the
original and eleven in the revised that are completely without illustrations or other concrete language. Of course, the revised chapter
is longer, but proportionally not this much longer. Likewise, concrete language is not the whole basis of literary merit; but Lewis
made it the foundation of poetry (in the larger sense) in the fifth
chapter of *The Personal Heresy,* and it is indicative here.

Miracles is in tone much like Lewis's early philosophic works,
discussed in the previous chapter. But the argument here is not on
the basis of a morality (with a moral God, whether or not mentioned,
behind it); but in terms of a supernatural Reason in which man's
reason participates. One remembers that in *The Pilgrim's Regress,*
dropping the allegorical images, the three things that Wisdom says
were not created by man were logical categories, moral rules, and
Sehnsucht. The Pilgrim's Regress was primarily the account of *Sehnsucht*
leading "John" to God; "Right and Wrong as a Clue to the Meaning
of the Universe" argued from morality to God; *Miracles* is arguing
from reason—logical categories—to God in these early chapters.
(Another reason Lewis may have stopped direct apologetics with
this book is that he had exhausted his three ways to God.)

Indeed, in chapter 5, "A Further Difficulty in Naturalism," Lewis
argues in terms of natural law here also, saying he sees man's moral
awareness as part of reason, although others in the natural law
tradition do not. Either way, it makes a parallel case: a naturalist
(in Lewis's sense) cannot argue for any moral principles because he
believes they have nonmoral and nonrational causes. But Schakel
comments, in *Reason and Imagination in C. S. Lewis* (135), that
Lewis's basic argument leaves open the position of skepticism: perhaps naturalism is the truth—but, if so, one has no rational means
of proving it.

At any rate, Lewis, after arguing for man's reason needing a
supernatural Reason in order to be valid, later in the book admits
that it is easier to argue for the Incarnation in historical terms than
philosophical, and he offers a new version of his now familiar dis-

junction between Christ's claims for himself, which if they are not true suggest madness ("rampant megalomania"), and the sanity of his moral teachings (chap. 14). In short, he argues for rational theism, instead of moral theism, and then tries briefly to shift the theism into Christianity.

But this is advancing too quickly. The latter part of the book does not, at first, give the impression of as tight an organization as the first part. Admittedly, chapters 7 and 8 make a unit, discussing whether or not nature is a system that admits miracles; but the sheer title of 9, "A Chapter not strictly Necessary"—on external nature as a fallen creature that will be redeemed—indicates the pattern. (Lewis's artistic presentation of redeemed nature appears in new Narnia in the last four chapters of *The Last Battle*.) The next chapter, " 'Horrid Red Things,' " as Lewis indicates at the end, eliminates rejections of Christian claims based on the imagery involved, but does not touch the miraculous per se. And the next, "Christianity and 'Religion,' " is about an idealistic pantheism—in the philosophy of Bruno, Spinoza, and Hegel; in more popular writings, of Wordsworth, Carlyle, and Emerson—which is Christianity's main religious rival in the modern, Western world. Even here, there is more pattern than appears from the mere topics; in this eleventh chapter, Lewis builds on the discussion of imagery in the tenth. This eleventh, with its emphasis on God being more specific, more factual, than the amorphous pantheistic deity, is the basis for Lewis's imagery in *The Great Divorce* of Heaven as being harder, more specific, than the ghosts who visit it from Hell—as Lewis contrasts ghosts and saints here.

But Lewis is leading toward chapter 14, "The Grand Miracle," which is a discussion of the Incarnation (including, but not limited to, the Resurrection) as being the basic miracle that is asserted by Christianity and by which all Christian miracles should be judged. He leads into this with the twelfth chapter, "The Propriety of Miracles," and the thirteenth, "On Probability." The twelfth turns on an analogy, borrowed from Dorothy L. Sayers' *Mind of the Maker* (1941), between God and creation on one hand and a writer and his book on the other. Arguments from analogy are notoriously fallible, but this one is meant more to indicate the significance of some miracles than prove a point. If a miracle is basic to the type of plot (of the universe), it is artistically included; if it is used deus ex machina or if it is incidental frills, it is not.

The first of "On Probability" turns out to be a refutation of David Hume's essay "Of Miracles" (1748); this, where another philosophical writer might have begun, Lewis includes as preparation for a statement on the probability of the Incarnation. But the more important part of the chapter is Lewis's establishment of a criterion for the judgment of the probability of miracles: "some innate sense of the fitness of things." By itself, this sounds absurd; but Lewis quotes the phrase from an authority of science—Sir Arthur Eddington—who is writing about certain areas of scientific beliefs. As Lewis points out, science often progresses by concentrating on irregularities (things that do not "fit") and explaining how they can be fitted into the overall pattern (or a new, larger pattern). Obviously, this is an excellent debater's ploy: the use of a term from the opponent's camp to support one's own hypothesis. Lewis applies the phrase to miracles and builds his transition to the last three chapters that present, and argue the fitness of, the basic miracle claimed by Christianity and two types of miracles that are related to it.

Thus far, this discussion has been primarily concerned with Lewis's ideas and their disposal, which is appropriate given the philosophical bent of the book. Two comparisons to his fiction have appeared, and more could be made. For example, at one point Lewis mentions the possibility of God having created several natures, several universes, unrelated to each other (chap. 2). Fictionally, the travel to and from Narnia illustrates this concept—or to and from Charn in *The Magician's Nephew*. Even the comment that these universes would seem supernatural to each other is illustrated in the ghostlike appearance of Tirian on Earth (in the fourth chapter of *The Last Battle.*)

Likewise, Lewis's predilection for referring to his friends appears here. Owen Barfield's *Poetic Diction* is praised and used in an argument (chap. 10). Adam Fox, one of the less significant Inklings, is given credit for comparing the imagery of God's appearance to Ezekiel not to nature but to machinery—to a dynamo (chap. 14). And Charles Williams (his name is not in the index) provides the epigraph to chapter 14. Autobiographically, Lewis's brief reference to Kirkpatrick, his one-time tutor, adds a detail about Kirkpatrick's reading to the account in *Surprised by Joy* (not in the index, chap. 10).

Finally, little has been said about the artistry beyond the organization and the lack of imagery in the revised third chapter, and the mentioning of the opening poem. Many other points could be made. Perhaps two illustrative examples will suggest part of Lewis's technique. After establishing man's reason as dependent on God's reason, Lewis compares it, in a separate paragraph, to a waterlily whose roots go down to the soil beneath the pond; then he suggests that, for the naturalist, the pond has no bottom (chap. 4). This image does not prove anything, but it does make the naturalist seem foolish. Even more delightful is the discussion of the mystics' use of negatives about God, which Lewis illustrates in a paragraph about a limpet who has a vision of man and describes him as having no shell, not being attached to a rock, and not surrounded by water. The later, nonmystical limpets decide that man (after a step or two) is "a famished jelly in a dimensional void" (chap. 11). There is again satire here, as often in Lewis; but the sheer wit is what is impressive.

Chapter Seven

The Christian Essayist

When Lewis's works of moral philosophy and apologetics have been sorted out, there still remain three books of a more general sort on religious topics. One of these—*The Screwtape Letters* (1942)—was Lewis's first very successful book in sales, and it earned him the cover of *Time* magazine on 8 September 1947. The other two— *Reflections on the Psalms* (1958) and *Letters to Malcolm: Chiefly on Prayer* (1964)—came later in Lewis's career, after he had given up arguing the Christian case.

One of the things that tie these books together is their informality. The title *Reflections* suggests more scattered insights than an argued case. And the first and the last of these books, indeed, are fictional epistles, something like Oliver Goldsmith's *Citizen of the World* in the eighteenth century. This informal tone does not deny some organization of the material, as will be discussed.

The Screwtape Letters has been the most successful of the three as literature, inspiring a minor genre of imitations (including Lewis's "Screwtape Proposes a Toast"). The other two books are probably not often read for literary reasons; but one often finds citations of *Letters to Malcolm* on biographical matters, such as Lewis's belief in Purgatory. As the last book prepared before his death for the general public, it has some significance as a statement of his final religious positions.

The Screwtape Letters (1942) and "Screwtape Proposes a Toast" (1959)

In 1942 Lewis published one of his most popular books, the fictional correspondence of a senior devil in the lowerarchy of Hell (Screwtape) to his nephew (Wormwood) who is a tempter in England just before and during the first part of World War II. Published seventeen years later, "Screwtape Proposes a Toast" is, as its title indicates, a speech, rather than a letter; it is given before a graduating class of the Tempters' Training School. Essentially the thirty-one letters in Lewis's book are moral essays, restating traditional positions; but their inverted point of view makes them fresh in their phrasing. For example, the fourteenth letter is on the true meaning of humility, as contrasted to the popular idea of it; the seventeenth is on gluttony, particularly the form of Gluttony of Delicacy, rather than excess; and the twenty-sixth, on unselfishness, in part contrasted to charity. Other topics, more specifically religious, appear—such as the Christian view of war in the fifth letter, and a discussion of prayer in the twenty-seventh. In general, the letters discuss the temptations of an individual. This is in contrast to "Screwtape Proposes a Toast," which emphasizes the moral (or immoral) state of society in which the tempters will be operating.

The fictionalizing, so far as the narrative development of the book is concerned, is most often limited to the opening paragraph of each letter. This narrative element is two-fold: the life of the "patient" (as Screwtape refers to Wormwood's temptee) in England, and the interplay between the two demons in their spiritual realm. The patient becomes a Christian as an adult convert (letter 2), has some problems with his mother (3), worries one night at the start of the war (5), falls in with some fashionable, sophisticated friends (10–12), repents during a walk in nature and has a renewal of grace (13), continues to attend one church (16), falls in love with a young Christian woman (22), joins in the Christian circle around his fiancée (24), behaves well during the first air raid on his city (30), and dies, and is saved, during a subsequent air raid (31). Some of these items sound abrupt in this sequence, but they are often prepared for. Discussion of sexual temptation and of disastrous marriages (18–20) precedes the patient's falling in love; a warning to Wormwood to keep his patient alive during some predicted heavy air raids, for he is not in danger of damnation at the time (28), precedes the death.

The demonic "plot" is parallel. Wormwood is promised "the usual penalties" when his patient converts (letter 2); Screwtape gives Wormwood a warning about trying to shift responsibilities over a matter of prayer (4); Wormwood becomes ecstatic over the patient's wartime worry (5); Wormwood experiences the patient's state of grace as an asphyxiating cloud around him (13); Screwtape explains away his inconsistent statements about love, which Wormwood has pointed out (19); Screwtape has settled a problem with the Secret

Police that Wormwood caused him, sends a booklet "on the new House of Correction for Incompetent Tempters," and then, toward the end of this letter, changes in form to a centipede, referring to Milton's account of Satan's serpentine transformation in *Paradise Lost* (22); Screwtape threatens Wormwood with becoming food if he does not damn the patient (30); and Screwtape hopes to eat Wormwood, or part of him, after he has lost his patient to salvation (31). Perhaps the main inconsistency in Lewis's depiction is the use of the threat of torture sometimes and of being eaten at others as Wormwood's punishment for failure. ("Screwtape Proposes a Toast" is consistent in its eating and drinking imagery.) Also, in light of Screwtape's comments about the demonic boredom related to humans' off-color stories (11) and sexual temptations (18), it is difficult to imagine how an uncle-nephew relationship that reached even the point of acknowledgment, such as theirs, came about; certainly it was not pleasure or love that spawned Wormwood.

An organization of the content of nearly half of the letters exists. In the twenty-third letter, Screwtape alludes to the formula in the Anglican baptism of things to be rejected—the World, the Flesh, and the Devil. (So far as America is concerned, the reference is to the 1928 *Book of Common Prayer*; the formula is dropped in the more recent revision by the Episcopal Church.) Screwtape says the first two have failed, and so the third must be tried. The World refers to the worldly friends of the tenth through the twelfth letters, cut off by the repentance of the thirteenth; the Flesh seems to refer to the gluttony of the seventeenth letter and the rather vague attacks on the patient's chastity in the eighteenth and the nineteenth, which attacks are stopped by God in the twentieth. Since demons have a policy of not directly revealing themselves at the present time, "the Devil" of the three temptations cannot be something as direct as a pact (like Dr. Faustus); it refers to corruptions of the patient's spirituality: the attempts to combine Christianity with another cause (letter 23), to develop spiritual pride in a Christian inner circle (24), to cause dissatisfaction with God's emphasis on cycles (25), to substitute unselfishness for charity (26), and to raise doubts about petitionary prayer (27). Thirteen letters out of thirty one are hardly an exhaustive thematic structure; but, when combined with the "plots," this structure provides the interplay of two different methods of organization to create a type of complex unity.

No doubt, the use of the World, the Flesh, and the Devil provides a type of universality to the contents (and presumably that was the intention); but the student of Lewis will find personal touches of the author in the book still. For example, the first letter tells Wormwood to avoid arguments, which arouse reason, and to fix his patient's attention on "the stream of immediate sense impressions"; inverted, the Christian should pay attention to the universal issues raised by reason—which is certainly typical of Lewis's rational Christianity. The twentieth letter has a description of each man's inner visions of at least two women—the one he would marry; the other "he desires brutally, and desires to desire brutally." This sounds rather Victorian in its two women, and it sounds like the adolescent, sadistic Lewis in the second description. (The phrasing is also chauvinistic in another sense: in "any human's heart . . . he" has these two visions. So women are not human.) The final letter has an interesting depiction of *Sehnsucht*: the patient, dead, sees the angels who have been guarding him, and they awaken memories in him—they are the explanation of his consciousness as a child of friends around him; their appearance is the recovery of the "central music in every pure experience." (Music, as was indicated in the first chapter, is one of the four marks of *Sehnsucht* in Lewis's writings.)

Lewis as a philologist appears in the book when Screwtape distinguishes between various meanings of "living in the present" (letter 15) or discusses two meanings of the word *real* (30); likewise, a shift in the meaning of *Puritanism* is noted (10) and confusion in the use of *my* (21). Perhaps these philological touches were cause enough for Lewis to dedicate the book to Tolkien. The connection between "Screwtape Proposes a Toast" and *Studies in Words* was discussed earlier.

The Screwtape Letters in its popularity suggests Lewis found the right rhetorical approach to make morality and a religious point of view lively. Anyone who has read Dr. Johnson's moral essays in *The Rambler* can see the difference. Overall, Lewis's book holds up well since its publication. There are a few faulty patches—such as the inner vision of two women that seems based on a masculine double standard, the pure and the fallen, and that is hardly universal. Some discussions, such as the eighteenth letter with its "dilemma" of faithful marriage or celibacy, have little significance to many secularists today. But most of the material for those who live by natural law (that is, a traditional moral code)—whether or not they are religious—has at least symbolic validity. "Screwtape Proposes a Toast," on the other hand, with its concern about the leveling nature of modern democracy, is arguing an old anti-Jacksonian position in the United States and, perhaps for that reason, seems less significant after twenty-five years than its parent volume after forty.

Reflections on the Psalms (1958)

After the defenses of Christianity published in the 1940s, Lewis returned to straightforward, nonepistolary prose on a Christian topic with *Reflections on the Psalms,* a little over ten years later. It is his one book directly on part of the Bible and, before it is through, his basic statement on the Bible.

The volume is casually organized. After an introductory chapter, Lewis discusses three sober topics in the Psalms: their calls for God to render judgment (chap. 2), their cursings of enemies (3), and their concept of death (4). Next come two happier topics: the Psalms' delight in God and His worship (5) and in His law (6). The next three chapters seem miscellaneous: one on the Psalms' denunciation of associating with or respecting prominent evil doers, with a last paragraph on their like denunciation of lying, gossiping, and other verbal sins (7); another on the Psalms' type of appreciation of nature (8); and the third, about Lewis's early difficulties over God's demand that He be praised (9). The final three present a developed explanation of symbolic (or predictive) readings of the Old Testament in light of the New: the first differentiates, not just working from biblical texts, between arbitrary back-readings and those where there is some real relationships between the passages and later events (10); the second explains Lewis's understanding of scriptural inspiration and, hence, Old Testament preparation for the New, as well as the New Testament authority for such an approach (11); and the last, the types of predictions of Christ found in the Psalms (12).

A reader may wonder if the book is not ending with an anticlimax in the last chapter when Lewis drops down from a discussion of the Christian implications of Psalm 8 to end with three paragraphs on symbolic readings of the self-righteousness in the Psalms, the curses in them, and a poetic time reference in one. But what Lewis is doing is two-fold, under the rational guise of making a few minor points to wrap up. First, he is giving the book some structural unity with a not-unusual tying together of motifs. For example, the second of these paragraphs refers to Psalm 137, the passage about murdering infants, which was first mentioned in the book's third chapter. For another, both of the other paragraphs refer to Plato, who has appeared often in the volume—for example, in the eighth chapter with a theology of creation and in the tenth with his account of the perfectly good man being killed in this world. Second, Lewis is quietly returning to his apologetic mode. The antepenultimate paragraph concludes with a four-sentence parenthesis that restates Lewis's favorite dilemma in favor of Christ's divinity: given what He says, He is either divine or mad. The ultimate paragraph concludes with an argument from man's inability to accept the passage of time that he is not ultimately made for it, and illustrates this with the analogy of an invented fish who is dissatisfied with the wetness of water. In this book, one may say that Lewis is not argumentative *to* the last but only *at* the last.

Many interesting discussions of one sort or another occur in the book. Rather than trace the topics indicated above in the chapters, perhaps one should consider Lewis's analyses of individual psalms as of more literary interest. Certainly these show Lewis the critic and sometimes the historian of literature. In the sixth chapter, " 'Sweeter than Honey,' " in his consideration of the Jewish attitude toward the Law, Lewis has two such analyses. Psalm 119 is the long poem on the topic of the Law; Lewis compares its form to the (far shorter) sestina among modern forms. (The abecedarius in English has been used mainly for light verse, so it is not surprising Lewis does not use it for the comparison.) The love the author expresses for the Law Lewis suggests might be like that which Chinese Christians converted from (probably) Confucianism—Lewis does not identify the belief—might feel; Lewis obviously is not thinking of modern Chinese communists, but the reference to the order in traditional Chinese culture is really a reference to the Tao, as Lewis discussed it in *The Abolition of Man*. The comparison here seems to be just for clarification, but Lewis's understanding of natural law— one moral code for all mankind—underlies it. A final point: Lewis's discussion of the Psalm's triple assertion that the Law is the truth leads him to use the Hebrew word for truth, *emeth*. In the final Narnian Chronicle, *The Last Battle*, Emeth is a Calormene who, despite his mistaken worship of Tash, is accepted into the new Narnia in the penultimate chapter. Presumably one way of phrasing the cause of his salvation is to say he followed the Tao. And Psalm

119, with its praise of the Jewish written Law, is (for Lewis) praising one variety of the same universal code.

This discussion of 119 has been largely in terms of content and its ties to Lewis's main concerns; the discussion of Psalm 19, in the same chapter, is more strictly literary. Lewis calls it "the greatest poem in the Psalter and one of the greatest lyrics in the world." He then analyzes its three-part structure and discusses the imagination that must lie behind the leap from the first to the second part.

One further example will have to suffice. In the eighth chapter, "Nature," Lewis compares Psalm 104 and the Egyptian "Hymn to the Sun," written by Akhenaten, and suggests that a monotheistic understanding of creation will inevitably produce parallels. But there is a slight touch of dualism in "The Hymn to the Sun": the lion, the serpent, the nighttime seem to be evil. Psalm 104 is able to celebrate God's creation of the lion and the whale, as well as the domestic and huntable animals. And there is a tie to Lewis's fiction: his comment that Akhenaten's religion may have been too rational to serve as the basis for God's approach to mankind is like Orual's discovery in *Till We Have Faces* (bk. 2, chap. 2) that the Greek statue of Aphrodite did not console her peasants in the way the shapeless sacrificial stone of Ungit did.

The book can be tied to Lewis's concerns in other ways than through his psalmic discussions. Although Dante is not mentioned, Charles Williams gets in for a generalization applied to the corruption of the Law (chap. 6). Typical of both Williams's and Lewis's emphases is the phrase from the Athanasian Creed, that the Incarnation was "not by the conversion of the godhead into flesh, but by taking of [the] manhood into God" (quoted in chap. 11). This is part of Lewis's discussion of his understanding of the inspiration of Scripture, and he is making the application that God raised literature (myth, poetry, chronicle, fiction) into Holy Scripture, with its various degrees of accuracy and purity. (Lewis's use of this phrase in *The Four Loves* was discussed in "The Moral Philosopher" chapter.)

It is in this chapter that Lewis contrasts his position with both the Fundamentalist's reliance on an infallible Bible and the Roman Catholic's, on an infallible Church. Lewis sums up the usual defense of their separate authorities in a syllogism, and then denies both the major and minor premises. Indeed, there is more of the Anglican

Lewis in *Reflections on the Psalms* than he usually allows himself: the discussion of the Psalms with double meanings in the last chapter is tied to their appearances in the Church Year in *The Book of Common Prayer*.

Other personal comments could be mentioned. For one example out of several, Lewis's reference to his reviewers finding ingenuous, unintended allegories in his fantasies is a pleasant touch (chap. 10). And perhaps a personal result should be mentioned: after this book appeared, Lewis was asked to serve as one of the seven members of the committee to revise the psalms for the Church of England. *The Revised Psalter* (1966) is not often listed as one of Lewis's books, but he, T. S. Eliot, and others were the modernizers of Coverdale's translation.

Lewis's style has not greatly changed from his other books. Dabney Hart, in *Through the Open Door* (1984), lists as one of the three major characteristics of his style mixed metaphors, by which she means quick shifts from one image to another as he illustrates a topic.[1] For example, Lewis compares obeying a law that restrains a strong, innocent desire to "approaching the dentist's forceps or the front line" (chap. 6). In this book, Lewis mentions how Jesus often ran two or three parallel images to make a point memorable, following "the poetic tradition of His country" (chap. 1). As Jesus probably learned the device from the Psalms, so Lewis—although Hart does not make the point—may have learned it from Christ.

Lewis is often provocative. His defense of having the nihilism of Ecclesiastes in the Bible is interesting (chap. 11). Lewis calls it "a clear, cold picture of man's life without God." (Lewis often quotes James Moffatt's translation in this book, and Moffatt brackets the most pious statements in Ecclesiastes as interpolations.) This comment on Ecclesiastes, instead of the Psalter, is the proper place to stop, for *Reflections on the Psalms* is, sometimes by brief reference and sometimes by full discussion, Lewis's book on the Bible—a summary of his approach to the Scriptures and the values (and other things) he found.

Letters to Malcolm, Chiefly on Prayer (1964)

His last completed book, written in the latter half of 1962 and the first of 1963, while he was ill, *Letters to Malcolm* is not Lewis's best work. It has some good writing, as always, but few of the topics are completely fresh. (An example, in the ninth letter, is mentioned below.) Lewis was obviously seeking a form that avoided authoritarianism—"for me to offer the world instruction about prayer would be impudence" (letter 12)—but his choice of letters to an invented friend allows for a very casual organization. Probably more people return to the volume for what it reveals of Lewis's personal beliefs than reread it for its comments on prayer. Even the subtitle suggests the casualness. The book is best seen aesthetically as the production of a serious Charles Lamb, writing mainly on one topic but ready to digress at any time and to divide up his essays between topics (something Elia in general did not do).

Thus, the organization of the twenty-two letters is casual. But one fairly obvious block of letters, from the fourth through the twelfth, is, with some digressions (mainly letters 6 and 10), on petitionary prayer. This block includes the main fictional episode in the book: in the eighth letter, George, the son of Malcolm and Betty, is diagnosed by a family doctor—a general practitioner—as having a serious illness. (Lewis never gives it a name, but X-rays are involved in the checking.) The ninth letter resolves the problem as a false diagnosis, as quickly as it arose; presumably Lewis's purpose in that eighth letter is to show the difference between the theorizing about prayer and the emotions when a dire situation calls for prayer. Since Lewis is supposed to be writing these letters once a week, the correction of the diagnosis by the time of the ninth letter is logical— although the present reader feels a loss of fictional development in the episode. The emotions called forth vanish too quickly into a discussion in the ninth letter of petitionary prayer as a causal agent (much the same approach as Lewis gives in Appendix B to *Miracles*).

Other types of prayer are discussed in the book. Lewis, in the first letter, refuses liturgical prayer as a main topic of the correspondence, making a few comments on it. The second mentions several means of personal prayer: use of prayers written by others, mental (mainly nonverbal) prayers, and prayers of one's own words. More strictly parallel to the topic of petitionary prayers are discussions of prayer as worship and adoration (letters 17 and 19) and of penitential prayer (18). These examples could be multiplied, but most interesting is that the end of the book wanders off the topic of prayer at all. The last letter is prepared for by the twentieth, in which Lewis discusses prayers for the dead, Purgatory, the time-lessness of God, and the possibly partial time-based existence of angels and souls. Then, in the twenty-second, Lewis discusses liberal Christians (not for the first time in this digressive book) and, with the pretense that Malcolm had commented on so much emphasis on the supernatural and the afterlife, imagines the resurrection of the body on the New Earth as the soul's containment of memory and the senses inside itself.

Even the above discussion does not indicate how many brief passages in these letters are on topics unrelated to prayer, but it may suggest the general nature of the book. Further, the use of replies to "Malcolm" or "Betty" permits Lewis to skip around in his topics. The placement of the letter on penitential prayer between the two on prayers of adoration indicates this. It is traditional to speak of "the art that conceals art"; here it might be more proper to say "the deliberate disorganization that conceals art."

On the other hand, the reader interested in Lewis's personal attitudes, however they are organized, will find a treasury in the volume. For example, Lewis says flatly here that he believes in Purgatory (letter 20). His belief in Purgatory had been mentioned in earlier works (e.g., *Reflections on the Psalms,* chap. 1), but this is the fullest statement. Dante is mentioned in this connection (as well as three other times). This passage may be used as an illustration of artistry. Lewis asserts his belief and then discusses the historic background that caused the Anglican Reformers to reject the doctrine of Purgatory in the Thirty-Nine Articles. After that bow to his tradition, Lewis quotes John Henry Newman (from a poem), showing a recovery of the true meaning of the doctrine, and concludes, "Religion has reclaimed Purgatory." *Religion* probably alludes to an earlier passage in this book in which Lewis lambasted Newman for using that word to mean *God* (letter 6); but, though Lewis allows Newman his term, here it can only mean something like "Church tradition," rather than the Deity. Having made his argument, Lewis backs it up with an imaginative dialogue between God and a saved soul and an image from dentistry. In short, this passage, like many others in the book, shows Lewis in rhetorical control of his material.

Other personal comments include two paragraphs on Lewis's desire to peep behind the spiritual scenes (letter 7), which presumably explain his doing it imaginatively in *The Screwtape Letters* and *The Great Divorce.* He quotes from Charles Williams twice, the first time without Williams's name (letters 14, 21); the second citation of

Williams—"Doesn't Charles Williams say someplace"—is part of Lewis's informality in this book, for he had quoted the passage in chapter 4 of "Williams and the Arthuriad" (1948) and given its source. But the personal element that may be most generally interesting is Lewis's references to his marriage to Joy Davidman: in the eighth letter are a few indications of his grief at her death; more positively, in the last letter, Lewis mentions unsought memories coming sometimes of their lovemaking, and he also refers to the idea of the soul spending its time until the Resurrection in "Lenten lands"—a phrase also used in Lewis's poem on the memorial tablet for Davidman's ashes.

Chapter Eight
The Romancer (I)

The fiction of C. S. Lewis consists of romances, not novels—that is, they are fantasies, not imitations of reality. Nathaniel Hawthorne, himself a romance writer, made the already-traditional distinction in his preface to *The House of Seven Gables* (1851), adding two restrictions. The first was a preference: the romancer should not stray too far from reality, although Hawthorne admitted there was no real law against it. Second, Hawthorne said that the romancer should remain true to "the human heart." This suggests that the romance should have some type of symbolic truth for the reader. Of course, the truth for Nathaniel Hawthorne and the truth for C. S. Lewis may not resemble each other; but if they are both human truths, they at least will suggest the complexity of the human situation.

This distinction between the two types of fiction has been restated recently by a prominent critic, Northrop Frye, who, in his *Anatomy of Criticism,* set up four types of fiction (all of equal validity, he said): novel, romance, anatomy (novel of ideas), and confession (303–14). In Frye's terms, Lewis remains a romance writer, although often, outside of the Narnian books, a writer of hybrids between the romance and other forms. *Till We Have Faces,* for example, fits what Frye calls a romance-confession.

Hawthorne and Frye are invoked here because often fantasies are rejected per se by those readers whose conditioning has been that of realism. But the present time, with some writers calling themselves postrealists, with the critical reputations of Kafka and Borges, with the late Italo Calvino in Italy and a number of romancers in Latin America, and with the public recognition in the Nobel Prize of Isaac Bashevis Singer—many of whose works are fantasies—should be a period open to the types of fantasies that Lewis wrote, among others.

Lewis also may be dismissed by some for being heavy-handed with Christian meanings. There are several answers to this. First, as Lewis noted in "Unreal Estates" (1964), his fiction began with

mental pictures, not with didactic intent. This does not deny didacticism, but it suggests that the books are not wholly intended
to teach or preach. Second, in "A Reply to Professor Haldane"
(1966), Lewis distinguished between *Out of the Silent Planet* and
Perelandra, saying the latter was written for his "co-religionists."
Thus, the amount of Christian discussion and imagery (not necessarily preaching, as it is sometimes taken to be) varies from book
to book. Third, in the most general sense, it is obviously true that
non-Christians can read Dante and Milton—and Lewis—with the
same type of "willing suspension of disbelief" that Christian readers
give to Lucretius or Thomas Hardy. If a non-Christian has trouble
doing that with Lewis because he was a mid-twentieth-century author rather than one of the fourteenth or seventeenth centuries, let
the reader recall Kathleen Raine's witty description in her essay
"Edwin Muir" of a twentieth-century "Anglican Revival";[1] let the
reader "place" Lewis historically with Charles Williams, Dorothy
L. Sayers, T. S. Eliot, and W. H. Auden, and other figures, and
enjoy him (if he turns out to be enjoyable) as part of a period. The
present writer believes that *Till We Have Faces,* preeminently, will
repay the effort.

Lewis's four short stories and two fragments of novels have been
ignored in this chapter and the next, as most of his essays have been
earlier.

Out of the Silent Planet (1938)

Lewis's first science-fiction romance, what may be called the first
of the Ransom Trilogy, arose from a desire by Lewis and Tolkien
to write mythopoeic thrillers—the type of book they enjoyed reading. Lewis finished a fiction of space travel and Tolkien began, but
did not finish, one of time travel. Lewis's essays "On Stories" (1947)
and "On Science Fiction" (1966) are good guides to what he intended, for the first, despite its title, is on prose romances. Two
points will do for a start: in "On Stories" Lewis comments that, for
him, a romantic setting and exotic culture are more important than
narrative thrills; in "On Science Fiction" he has a passing suggestion
that H. G. Wells's Cavor and Bedford in *The First Men in the Moon*
are too complex in personality: "Every good writer knows that the
more unusual the scenes and events of his story are, the slighter,
the more ordinary, the more typical his persons should be."

In *Out of the Silent Planet*, then, there is much description of Mars ("Malacandra") with two of its cultures, and the three main humans are type characters: Weston, the amoral scientific humanist; Devine, the seeker of wealth and pleasure; and Ransom, the focal character, a pious, middle-aged Cambridge philologist—despite his (assumed) learning, a person fairly average in his reactions to events. (It is typical of the genre that Ransom sounds more learned and thus less average in the letter that appears as the postscript to the book than he does in any of the earlier chapters.)

For the plot, one may begin with Northrop Frye's comment that the essential plot of a romance is a sequence of adventures (186–87). Ransom, on a walking tour, is kidnapped by Weston and Devine and taken to Mars to be given to the *sorns* (very tall, white, feather-covered beings). He escapes and, after some wandering, reaches the society of the *hrossa* (black-haired animals of about human size), where he learns one of the three languages of Mars and joins, ultimately, the hunt for a large lake serpent. Up to this point, the plot can be described as that of the "reluctant quest." But, after Ransom's closest friend among the *hrossa* is shot by Weston and Devine, he chooses to obey the instruction of an *eldil* (an angel-like being) and journeys to meet Oyarsa (the Intelligence of the planet) on an island Meldilorn, going by way of a mountain pass and staying with *sorns* for two nights on the way. It is typical of Lewis's temperamental balance between the romantic and the argumentative (the latter tied to Frye's concept of the anatomy as a type of fiction) that the meeting at the end of the quest, while prepared for by romantic imagery—"Amidst the lake there rose like a low and gently sloping pyramid, or like a woman's breast, an island of pale red" (chap. 17)—that the meeting is an ironic presentation of Weston's ideas.

An illuminating discussion of this as science-fiction is by Mark R. Hillegas: he points out that Lewis's spaceship is based on that used in Wells's *The First Men in the Moon* (1901) and that the interview with Oyarsa on Meldilorn is based on the interview with the Grand Lunar in Wells's book—which in turn is based on Gulliver's interview with the King of Brobdingnag in Jonathan Swift's *Voyages* (1726).[2] Lewis, after an introductory note praising Wells, refers to the fears of aliens created in Ransom's mind by Wells's writings (chaps. 5, 11). In short Lewis writes *Out of the Silent Planet* in Wells's tradition, although with his own religious and philosophical bias, as would be expected. And it is not just Wells who is being used here. One of Weston's statements in his own defense, praising his attempts to preserve and extend the human race—"it is enough for me that there is a Beyond" (chap. 20)—is, if "for me" is left out and "beyond" is spelled in lower case, the final sentence of George Bernard Shaw's *Back to Methuselah* (1921). (Lewis also pilloried the celebration of human life, without regard to its morality, in his "Evolutionary Hymn" [1957], which echoes some of Weston's language in chap. 20.) These references to Wells and Shaw tie Lewis to his time, of course; but they also suggest his fiction is within at least one of the intellectual currents of the twentieth century—within it, as a response, or cross-current, to it.

In "A Reply to Professor Haldane," Lewis comments that the science in *Out of the Silent Planet* is not intended to be perfectly accurate. He used canals on Mars, for example, because they were part of the popular picture of that planet, not because they were still believed in by scientists in 1938. Lewis also notes that, although he has to be a physicist for plot purposes (to have developed the spaceship), Weston talks little but biological, or "metabiological," theory. Other illustrations are easy to produce. For one example, the sun seems to fill the space with brightness (which is incorrect), and in one passage Ransom thinks that this brightness ends with the edge of the solar system (chap. 6)—as if the sun's radiation suddenly stopped at that point. This *may* be intended to characterize the lack of scientific knowledge of Cambridge philologists in the 1930s. Or, more likely, this is intended to use Ransom's "ignorance" to recreate some of the effect of the medieval view of the solar system. At the very end of the volume, in the postscript, Ransom refers to the Malacandrians "turning the solar system inside out," as if the sun were its outer edge and the large planets closer to its center, and to their emphasis on Jupiter. The significance of Jupiter is summed up in Lewis's description of the medieval world view in *The Discarded Image,* as is the brightness of the solar system, and the inverted solar system probably comes from the vision of the angelic Intelligences in Dante's *Il Paradiso,* canto 28 (cited in *The Discarded Image*—all chap. 5, sec. B). In short, the science in *Out of the Silent Planet* is often used with a romancer's hand, not a realist's.

Most explicators today spend much time on the Christian background implicit in the book, but few of the early reviewers noticed it—which suggests it is more thoroughly background than most of today's writers acknowledge. In theological terms Lewis is describing an unfallen, sinless world under the direction of an angelic Intelligence. The *eldila,* visible only with difficulty, are angels. In the case of the *eldil* who comes walking across water to Ransom during the *hnakra* hunt (chap. 13), the *eldil* functions as a traditional angelic messenger (with the aded touch of echoing Christ's walking on water). Lewis also, however, provides a "scientific" explanation of *eldila* as beings existing at the energy level of light, and thus finding different things solid and infirm than do humans and Malacandrians (chap. 15). In one passage, a *hross* explains that Maleldil the Young (i.e., Christ) made and rules the world, and lives with the Old One (i.e., God the Father) (chap. 11). But non-Christians, who do not tend to think of God the Son outside of his earthly incarnation, would probably miss the reference—and it is appropriate that a Malacandrian would not know of the Incarnation. The word *Maleldil* is misleading, because many readers, meeting it for the first time, probably associate *mal-* with evil. (Actually, Lewis seems to have derived the word from Anglo-Saxon, *mal* [an agreement, a judgment] or *mael* [a sign] + *ealdor* [lord]; hence, Lord of the Sign, Lord of Judgment, or Lord of the Agreement/Covenant.)[3] Of these Christian motifs, probably the angels (with the "War in Heaven" explanation for Earth being the "silent planet") are the most obvious; but none of the material is didactic in any direct way.

Indeed, if one wants a classification for *Out of the Silent Planet* besides "science-fiction romance," the term is *not* "Christian didacticism" but "religious Utopia." (Many of the early Utopian works were also religious in orientation—as were many of the early Utopian communities in America.) One critic has suggested that Lewis belongs to a reaction against H. G. Wells's Utopian works, such as *A Modern Utopia* (1905) and *Men Like Gods* (1923);[4] another, that the three types of Malacandrians—the *pfifltriggi, hrossa,* and *séroni* (or *sorns*)—parallel the three classes in Plato's *Republic*—the workers, guardians (in Lewis, just a group that emphasizes physical bravery), and philosophers.[5] In this light, it is fitting that Oyarsa, in answering Weston's beliefs, does *not* say, "Thus saith the Lord," but instead replies in terms of natural law: he refers to the laws that all *hnau* (intelligent beings) know, including the love of kindred, and says that Weston substituted that one lesser moral law for all the others (chap. 20). In short, Lewis's emphasis on the fallen nature of mankind in this book serves as foil to establish the Platonic-and-pre-Christian religious (or natural law) Utopia of Malacandra.

Perelandra (1943)

When Lewis wrote in "A Reply to Professor Haldane" that *Perelandra* was intended for his "co-religionists," he indicated its limitations. Of course, the romance is nicely plotted and the watery world of Venus with its floating islands (as imagined before the current knowledge of the Venerian surface temperature) is very well described. But an agnostic science-fiction fan, for example, is not likely to make the book a personal touchstone of the field and return to it again and again, as he or she might to (say) Edgar Pangborn's *Davy* (1964). On the other hand, one of Lewis's Christian readers might consider it the best of Lewis's fictions and read it many times through the years, partially because of the portrait of true, but not naive, purity. For Lewis has described that cliché in science-fiction circles (perhaps he began it): an Adam and Eve on a new world. More specifically, Ransom journeys to Venus (Perelandra) in order, he discovers, to help the Venerian Eve resist the Tempter. As an early critic wittily said, *Perelandra* is a Paradise Retained.[6]

The Miltonic allusion is just, for Lewis wrote this book at approximately the same time as *A Preface to "Paradise Lost"* (the publication dates are within a year of each other). As might be expected, several critics have compared Lewis's nonfiction study of Milton's poem with *Perelandra*;[7] for present purposes, the acknowledgment of the Miltonic influence, with Lewisian modifications based on comments about Miltonic weaknesses, is sufficient. Perhaps, if *Out of the Silent Planet* is called a science-fiction romance, this second of the Ransom Trilogy should be called an archetypal romance. Certainly Tinidril as Eve;[8] Weston, now the Un-man (chap. 9), as a devil; and Ransom, despite his human weaknesses, as participating in the physicality, the Incarnation, of Jesus ("My name also is Ransom" [chap. 11]), are religious archetypes. Northrop Frye writes in terms of the romance using psychological archetypes—his examples are Jungian (304)—but these will do to show the generic class, at least.

Unlike *Out of the Silent Planet*, which ended with a chapter by the fictional Lewis and a postscript letter by Ransom, the half-frame in

Perelandra comes first: two chapters that tell, from "Lewis's" first-person point of view, of Ransom's departure to Venus and his return. The use of a white coffinlike box moved by Oyarsa, instead of a spaceship, serves two purposes: it varies the books, and it indicates that this volume is much more fantasy than science fiction. There are other differences as Lewis restructures some materials for his new intentions: for one example, *Oyarsa* seemed a name in *Out of the Silent Planet*, but now the Intelligence is usually called "the Oyarsa of Malacandra" (chap. 1, italics omitted), or suitable variations, making the personal name into a title.

Ransom's adventures on Venus are more tightly structured than were those on Mars, Lewis consciously or unconsciously using the pattern of what is critically called Freytag's Pyramid. The exposition (chaps. 3–7) introduces Ransom to the floating islands, to Tinidril, and to the Fixed Land where Tinidril is commanded by Maleldil not to sleep; and Weston, possessed by a (or the) devil, shows up in a new spaceship. Weston's arrival may be called the activating circumstance (Freytag's inciting moment) that changes a potential conflict into a real one. The temptation of Tinidril, with the arguments and other forms of persuasion by the Un-man and Ransom (chaps. 8–10), is the rising action. These arguments are, in Northrop Frye's terms, an anatomy portion of this romance (cf. his comments on the short form of the anatomy [310–11]). Frye also calls the romance-anatomy hybrid "a rare and fitful combination" (314). Presumably few authors are as balanced between the romantic and the argumentative as is Lewis, but even here the fiction tends to shift back and forth, rather fusing the two.

The turning point of the plot is chapter 11, in which Ransom comes to the realization that it is not enough to argue; he must use force to defeat the Un-man. This has been prepared for. Tinidril, although green in color, is human in form because of Maleldil's Incarnation on Earth: thus, the Incarnation has been an important theological change (e.g., the various forms of rational beings on Mars are no longer permissible in new parts of the universe). Further, as Satan (in Milton's poem) entered the serpent to tempt Eve, so here he (or one of his fellows) has entered Weston to reach Venus and tempt Tinidril. Ransom has been brought bodily to the planet. All of this prepares for the bodily combat. Lewis also alludes in this chapter, in Ransom's thoughts, to World War II going on on Earth at this time—also a physical combat. The war reference, no doubt, reached at the time some readers who would have otherwise felt that the book was losing its "spiritual" level.

The falling action is the physical fight of Ransom and the Un-man, beginning on the floating island; their chase on fish-mounts to a second Fixed Land; and Ransom's first "killing" of the Un-man by strangulation in a cavern (chaps. 12 through the beginning of 14). The resolution is elaborated: first, the real killing of the Un-man (the end of chap. 14); second, Ransom's recovery by a pool, eating grapelike fruits and sleeping (the first of chap. 15)—probably echoing the well of life (baptism) and the tree of life (communion) that restores the Redcrosse Knight after his first two days of battle with the dragon in Edmund Spenser's *Faerie Queene* (bk. 1, can. 11, sts. 29–46); third, Ransom's climbing of a high mountain nearby, his meeting in the flowery meadow on top the Intelligences of Mars and Venus, Tor (the Perelandrian Adam), and the unfallen Tinidril, and, after a mystical vision of the Great Dance, his preparing to return to Earth (the rest of chap. 15 through 17). In Lewis's essay "Shelley, Dryden, and Mr. Eliot" (1939), he praises the fourth act of *Prometheus Unbound,* which is added to the completed action of the play and which is "sustained on the note of ecstasy such as no other English poet, perhaps no other poet, has given us." No one would argue that the liturgical praises of Maleldil that pass into the vision of the Great Dance in the last chapter of *Perelandra* are at Shelley's level as Lewis perceives it; but surely Lewis is attempting something of the same type in his prose. The plot does not call for the vision, but the vision illumines the type of mystical knowledge that resistance to sin has allowed.

Spenser and Shelley, however, are not ultimately basic to the last part of the book, nor is Milton; Dante is. Perhaps the use of Dantean imagery is prepared for by a suggestion that Weston's soul is in Hell, while a devil animates his body in this universe (chaps. 10, 13), as Dante, the character, sees the soul of Ser Branca d'Oria in Hell while his body is still on Earth (*Inferno,* canto 33). But it is the general image of *The Divine Comedy* that is important here, as it is at the end of *Till We Have Faces*: Hell, or the Inferno, as a journey through a cavern beneath the earth; the climbing of Mount Purgatory and reaching the Garden of Eden on top; Heaven, or the Paradiso, as the journey through the heavens with the Beatific Vision at the end.

Ransom symbolically dies—that is, he nearly drowns—as he

enters the underground caverns (chaps. 13–14). In these caverns, this Hell, he has his struggle with the Un-man, a devil. Ultimately, he uses a rock to crush his head and throws his body into a fiery pit (chap. 14). The other touches show this to be a potential Hell, not an actual one, since Tinidril did not fall: the crustaceanlike monster that accompanies the Un-man at the last killing does not turn out to be evil; the two great thrones, perhaps for the likes of Pluto and Proserpina, are empty; the figure on a flat car, drawn by four crustaceans, is mantled and hence not revealed to the upper inhabitants of Perelandra (chap. 15). (The booming of drums that follows may be influenced by Tolkien's account of Moria in *The Lord of the Rings,* not yet published but written and read to Lewis that far.)

In chapter 15, when Ransom emerges, one of the things of which he is soon aware is a song, which turns out to be produced by a shy beast about the size of a small elephant; it is not very like, but perhaps it is meant to parallel, the song of Casella at the base of Mount Purgatory (*Purgatorio,* canto 2). At any rate, Ransom climbs "the great mountain," pausing to sleep during the one night of his climb, as Dante could not advance during his three nights on Mount Purgatory (cantos 7, 17, 27). Ransom reaches the top, which has ten or twelve peaks covered with red lilies, surrounding a valley of a few acres, also covered with red lilies and with a pond in its center—Ransom enters, with an allusion to the angel's sword guarding the Garden of Eden, as Dante passes through a wall of flame (the red lilies are the substitute for the flames, since there is no purgation of sin on Perelandra) and enters the Garden of Eden, where he finds red and yellow flowers and a stream (canto 28). On the unfallen world, it is appropriate that Tor and Tinidril appear in this Eden (chap. 16), unlike the fallen world of *Il Purgatorio* where two saved souls—Matilda and Beatrice—have to come down to greet Dante.

Il Paradiso is suggested in two ways. First, the vision of the Great Dance is a substitution for the Beatific Vision that ends Dante's poem, particularly the part in Dante connecting substance, accidence, and mode (canto 32); both visions fade out at the end. Second, transposed from Dante's sequence, the preparation at the end for Ransom's flight into space suggests the beginning of *Il Paradiso,* when Dante is lifted into the Ptolemaic space of his universe (canto 1). It is no wonder Lewis put Ransom's return in the second chapter:

to have used it as a frame at the end of the book would have reduced the significance of the imagery.

Perhaps it is useful for the reader to remind him- or herself that there will be greatly different reactions to this book and these images. Clyde S. Kilby, a Christian writer and academician, speaks of the conclusion as "a scene of unparalleled glorious ceremony."[9] However, a dissertation writer who is discussing science fiction and who demonstrates that he understands the meaning of *Perelandra* well, comments, "The novel is greatly weakened . . . by its ending, which seems rather to froth at the mouth in religious ecstasy. . . . One can almost apprehend the flow of spittle."[10] He seems to be referring to the liturgy before the vision and, given Lewis's Anglican background in *The Book of Common Prayer*, seems unjust in his assumptions about how the liturgy would be "read"—but it is his reaction itself that is revealing. Lewis was right about the volume being (mainly) for his coreligionists.

That Hideous Strength (1945)

The third volume of the Ransom Trilogy, *That Hideous Strength: A Modern Fairy-Tale for Grown-Ups,* is an olla podrida, a savory stew for those who like romances but certainly an odd mixture of ingredients. Almost no one will like every bite, and some of the mixture argues for a flaw in the cook who thought to combine its foodstuffs. More literally, the book is not a simply structured and successful work like *Out of the Silent Planet*; it is a complexly structured partial success.

A brief discussion of the five sections of the first chapter, "Sale of College Property," can illustrate the mixture. The first section is a third-person view of Jane Studdock one morning: she is a young married woman, trying to work on her doctoral dissertation but unable to concentrate; she is also, this being a romance, psychic, and she finds an account in a newspaper of the French execution of a man she had dreamed of the previous night. The second section is a similar view of Mark, Jane's husband; the setting is identified as Bracton College in Edgestow. The narrator (presumably the fictional Lewis of the previous volumes but never identified) adds some comments about the beauty of Edgestow, mentioning the four colleges that make up the University—the three men's colleges by name and "the nineteenth-century women's college beyond the railway." (Any feminist will find *That Hideous Strength* greatly irritating, particularly in the treatment of Jane Studdock; this passage is symptomatic—of British society, as Virginia Woolf's comments about women's colleges in *A Room of One's Own* [1929] make clear, as well as of Lewis.) Mark, an academic sociologist, is involved in college politics. Mark's desire to be in the inner circle is the type of folly discussed by Lewis in "The Inner Ring" (1949); presumably, as he said was true of all the sins he denounced (SJ, chap. 7), it was a compulsion that Lewis felt. This section is also used to introduce the name of Lord Feverstone, the Dick Devine of *Out of the Silent Planet,* who appears in person in the fourth section; this is simply one of the several means of tying the trilogy together.

The third section shifts to a first-person reminiscence of a visit to Bragdon Wood, a mile-wide walled woodland owned by Bracton College across the Wynd River; a well with late British-Roman masonry, called Merlin's Well, is in the center. Lewis's description of the approach to the well through three college courtyards is a deliberately controlled sequence; his awareness in *A Preface to "Paradise Lost"* of Milton's use of the technique for the gradual approach to the Garden of Eden (chap. 7) is parallel. The fourth section is a description of a college meeting that takes most of a day; the telling is without a focal character, although Mark is present. At the end of the politically managed meeting, most of Bragdon Wood, including the well, has been sold to the National Institute of Coordinated Experiments (usually referred to in the book by its ironic initials, the N.I.C.E.). The fifth section follows Jane and her thoughts as she goes into town, buys a hat, and ends up lunching with the Dimbles, he being one of her former university tutors. Lewis uses Cecil Dimble's mealtime conversation about Arthurian matters as an expository device, but Jane's tears before lunch and near-faint at the end of it are equally relevant to the fiction.

The foregoing, discussing just the first of seventeen chapters, suggests the diversity of materials—and Ransom and the Oyéresu (a new plural of *Oyarsa*) have not yet appeared. Perhaps the most delightful of the shifts in point of view in the book is the first half of the third section of chapter 14, which follows the semithoughts of Mr. Bultitude, a bear. But the main structure of the book is the—sometimes parallel—adventures of Jane and Mark Studdock.

In the second chapter, Lord Feverstone invites Mark to join the N.I.C.E. (sec. 1) while the Dimbles suggest Jane—because of her visions—visit a Miss Ironwood at St. Anne's on the Hill (chap. 1, sec. 5; chap. 2, sec. 2). The third chapter recounts their reactions to these two places: Mark's attempts to find out what his job would be (secs. 1, 2, 4), Jane's reaction against Grace Ironwood's acceptance of her visions as visions (sec. 3). If there is balance at the end of the chapter it is between Jane's freedom to leave St. Anne's (sec. 5) and William Hingest's decision to permanently leave the N.I.C.E. (sec. 4)—only to be murdered on his way back to Edgestow (chap. 3, sec. 4). The reaction of Hingest, a chemist at Bracton, so Lewis commented in "A Reply to Professor Haldane," was put in to show that the N.I.C.E. was not a scientific institution; but the structure seems just as important.

In the fourth chapter appears the first of several passages in which Jane states to herself her basic desire to not be interfered with, to be left alone (sec. 5). Lewis mentions several times in *Surprised by Joy* his similar desire, so Jane, even more certainly than Mark, is based on Lewis's own emotions. Of course, Lewis has tied in fictional details that he, a bachelor at the time of the writing and a male, could hardly have experienced very directly: Jane's dislike of sexual union with Mark (euphemistically called "being kissed") and her decision not to have children yet (both chap. 1, sec. 5).

In chapter 5, Mark realizes he is trapped in the N.I.C.E.—if he loses his (vague) position there, he will also lose his fellowship at Bracton (sec. 2); Jane, on the other hand, refuses to join the Company at St. Anne's but does offer, freely, to tell them of any further dreams (sec. 3). The next chapter juxtaposes Mark's growing involvement in the N.I.C.E. (secs. 1–4) and Jane's decision to go to St. Anne's upon seeing on a street a N.I.C.E. official who had been studying her in her dreams (sec. 5).

At this point, chapters 7 and 9 must be taken as a balanced unit, with 8 as a transition between them. In 7, Jane meets Ransom (now, through an absurd explanation in chap. 5, sec. 3, Mr. Fisher-King). "Jane looked; and instantly her world was unmade" (the latter clause is repeated twice more). What is happening here needs to be explicit. Lewis, influenced by Charles Williams, is describing what Williams called the Beatrician revelation. As Dante looked on Beatrice, as recounted in *La Vita Nuova,* and fell completely in love, so Jane falls in love with Ransom.[11] Through this commitment will come others, and Jane will no longer live for herself. Further, Ransom, who in this book is a heightened picture of Williams, does what Lewis in a letter says that Williams did: he takes the love of female disciples and redirects it appropriately—in Jane's case, to her husband (LCSL, 208). On the other hand, in chap. 9, Mark's experience is not out of Dante and Williams; rather, he meets the balancing figure to Ransom, the head of the N.I.C.E. This is the literal human head of the French criminal Jane "saw" guillotined in the first chapter, kept alive scientifically, skull split open to allow further brain growth; but actually a "macrobe" (chap. 12, sec. 4)—that is, a devil—speaks through the Head. Here again Lewis may be writing mainly to his coreligionists, but the popular success of such Gothic romances as Ira Levin's *Rosemary's Baby* (1967) suggests that the devil is an acceptable figure in such fiction. Hawthorne's "Young Goodman Brown" and Singer's "Gentleman from Cracow" show that such stories can meet critical acceptance.

Structurally, these two meetings are parallel; both occur in the first sections of their respective chapters. But Mark's meeting with the head, while prepared for in chapter 8, section 3, is only recounted by Jane as occurring in one of her dreams, and it is not at the same thematic level as her meeting with Ransom: although it makes Mark sick, it does not change his life. His shifts in moods and attitudes are more extreme in the rest of that chapter and the next, but that is all.

In chapter 11, Jane and Mark face death. As she, because of her psychic powers, guides Cecil Dimble and another of St. Anne's Company in the search for Merlin (who has awakened), Jane thinks of death, because Merlin may be dangerous, and then of God (sec. 1); she does not get far before the action stops her. Mark, having been arrested for Hingest's murder after he too fled from the N.I.C.E., thinks of death in a cell (sec. 3). Unlike the meetings, here it is Mark's experience that is more important: he sees the past folly of his life. Jane's thoughts do not get to a turning point—or rather, with the meeting with Ransom, they already have.

The type of spirituality that reaches Mark leads not very directly toward theism, but to moral standards, something not inculcated in him before (chap. 9, sec. 2; chap. 14, sec. 1). In short, when he is taken from his cell (he has been returned to the N.I.C.E. headquarters), his path is parallel to that of Lewis. He discovers natural law, particularly as Lewis described it in *The Abolition of Man* (cf. the preface to *That Hideous Strength*). Mark reacts against the Objective Room (chap. 15, sec. 4) in which he is placed, with its irregular patterns and unnatural and antireligious pictures (chap. 14, sec. 1); he decides he believes in the Normal (also chap. 14, sec. 1), later termed the Straight (chap. 14, sec. 4) or the Wholesome (chap. 15, sec. 4). A philosophical conversion from a vague modernism, in brief.

That Hideous Strength has several times been called a Charles Williams novel by C. S. Lewis. This is not true, close as it may come, because ultimately Lewis does not allow the main characters to avoid a clear-cut Christian commitment. Williams's characters are in a moral, supernatural universe but usually not an explicitly Christian one. Lewis is, however, not satisfied with Jane's Beatrician experience. Ransom tells Jane she needs to become a Christian, in a discussion that turns partly on her feminine pride and resentment of the masculine per se (chap. 14, sec. 5); this is followed by a religious experience, a meeting with God and the origin of all demands, in the garden of St. Anne's (chap. 14, sec. 6). Likewise, Mark is not allowed to stay at the level of natural law. His training in the N.I.C.E. to not believe in a value system—which, as indicated above, had the opposite effect—climaxes in a demand that he trample on a realistic crucifix laid on the floor (chap. 15, sec. 4); admittedly, Mark is not converted at this point, but he sees it as a symbol "of what the Crooked did to the Straight"—thus identifying Christ as at least a representative of natural law.

The conclusion of the book reunites Mark and Jane—or, rather, ends the moment before they are reunited (chap. 17, sec. 8). Thus, the double plot fuses. As the passages near the end of the romance indicate, Jane has learned humility and obedience (chap. 17, sec. 8), and Mark has learned "the humility of the lover" (chap. 17, sec. 7)—for the final parallel before the end. Ransom's dismissal of Jane to go to her husband also resolves a problem by suggesting her psychic dreams will end either if she obediently loves Mark or if she has children (chap. 17, sec. 7)—the phrasing is ambiguous.

Structurally, the double plot works well, clear enough to be seen, not so rigid as to seem artificial. The Christian turns are forced; but, since *Out of the Silent Planet*, Lewis's reputation had been made with *The Screwtape Letters*, his early Christian apologetics, and *Perelandra*. And, no doubt, the explicit pointing was agreeable to his temperament.

Lewis's decision to use Arthurian materials was probably due to the influence of Charles Williams, whose first book of Arthurian poems, *Taliessin through Logres* (1938), is quoted (chap. 9, sec. 3), and a passage of whose Christian study, *He Came Down from Heaven* (1938), is alluded to (chap. 17, sec. 4). Indeed, Merlin refers to an Emperor over the West (chap. 13, sec. 5); although Merlin went to sleep with the Eastern Roman Empire not fallen, and hence under a theoretic imperial rule, probably the reference is due to Williams's use of the Emperor in *Taliessin through Logres* and *A Region of Summer Stars* (1944).

This indebtedness to Williams is part of what one critic has referred to as Lewis's attempt to sum up everything personally important to him until the time of writing in this book (Carpenter, 198). Lewis five times refers to Tolkien's Númenor, spelling it Numinor, which he identifies with Atlantis; this is, in general, appropriate, for "Akallabêth" in Tolkien's *Silmarillion* tells of the submersion of Númenor, called Atalantë in the Quenya language. Owen Barfield's anthroposophist ideas are referred to: the "ancient unities" before modern intellectual divisions of concepts (chap. 12, sec. 5), and spiritual evolution as a process of individualization (without Barfield mentioned, chap. 13, sec. 4). (In contrast, in *Perelandra* Barfield appears in the book as a character, when "B.," identified as an anthroposophist, manages one paraphrased statement in a discussion with Ransom [chap. 3].)

Besides Williams's use of Dante, two references to the *Inferno* help establish the climate of the N.I.C.E.: an allusion to one of the leaders of the N.I.C.E. as a soul who has "lost the intellectual good" (chap. 10, sec. 2), which echoes Virgil's words to Dante at Hell Gate about those who are damned (canto 3); and a later reference to another one of the leaders who was full of (spiritual and intellectual) sleep when he left the way (chap. 16, sec. 4), echoing Dante's description of his own straying (canto 1). These two allusions to Hell tied to the N.I.C.E. are part of its thematic identification.

Many other matters could be mentioned. Perhaps one autobiographical element and a few echoes of the period can be allowed to stand for all. One of the characters at the N.I.C.E., the head of the secret police, is a sadistic woman called "Fairy" Hardcastle. Since she seems to like to torture women (she burns Jane with a lit cigar a number of times, chap. 7, sec. 4), she is presumably a lesbian as the nickname suggests, taking out her sexual desires in physical pain. But she is also, one assumes, as was suggested earlier, a disguised version of Lewis's own teenage streak of sadism. She is not an unconscious projection on his part, for the book suggests a carefully and consciously controlled fiction; rather, she is (despite her womanhood) a picture of the sort of man Lewis could have become, if he had not chosen to control that side of his personality. A number of matters tie this book to its period. For example, five times Lewis substitutes as a swearword *bucking* for the obviously intended *fucking*; one remembers that such a realist as Norman Mailer in *The Naked and the Dead* (1948), three years after Lewis's book, substituted *fuggin* for *fucking*. Horace Jules, the nominal head of the N.I.C.E., is an obvious caricature of H. G. Wells (chap. 15, sec. 5): a Cockney, a popular journalist, a person given to good living, and one out of date in his science by the supposed after-the-war time of the novel. (Wells actually died in 1946, but Lewis finished the book in 1944.)

Another example: one of the members of the N.I.C.E. is Professor Filostrato, a very fat physiologist, who speaks with an Italian accent (chap. 3, sec. 2); he seems at first an ironic figure, for this fat man turns out to advocate the ultimate elimination of organic life from the planet (chap. 8, sec. 3). Then he appears more sinister than ironic: he is keeping the dead man's head alive, at least physically, as a symbol of the nonorganic, mental life to come (chap. 8, sec. 3; chap. 9, sec. 1). At one level, Filostrato is a parody of such antiphysical celebrations of the pre-World War II period as Shaw's conclusion to *Back to Methuselah,* where the evolved humans become vortices of energy, giving up their bodies. At another level, he, in his experiment of keeping the head alive—combined with the references to vivisection of animals at the N.I.C.E. (e.g., chap. 5, sec. 1)—reflects Lewis's objections recorded in "Vivisection" (1947). Finally, Filostrato's experiment with the head—this time combined with Fairy Hardcastle's uniformed officers (chap. 7, sec. 4) and power to "educate" human prisoners (chap. 14, sec. 5)—suggests the Nazi prison camps and Dr. Mengeles. Lewis probably did not know the details of the camps when he was writing in 1944, but rumors may have reached him. Certainly, the choice of an Italian physiologist would have carried associations with the Axis forces for the early readers.

This section on *That Hideous Strength* easily could be doubled in length; the overthrow of the N.I.C.E. by Merlin and the astrological Oyéresu has not been discussed, for example. But many of the significant ingredients of the stew have been nibbled; it is a romantic concoction, indeed.

The Great Divorce (1945)

The Great Divorce: A Dream appeared late in 1945. In 1944 Lewis read at least part of the book at Inklings' meetings. Since Lewis had the idea for this book in 1932, why did he finally produce it after twelve years? The cause may have been the Dantean influence of Charles Williams—and a Dantean interest at the time of Tolkien. The latter's "Leaf by Niggle" (1945) was written in 1943;[12] despite Tolkien's announced aversion to allegorical works,[13] it is an allegory with a few touches from Dante's *Divine Comedy,* especially "the Spring in the heart of the Forest," which is a modified version of the Lethe and Eunoë fountain on top of Dante's Mount Purgatory. In *The Great Divorce,* the fountain is not seen, but referred to ("A little like Lethe"); thus, all three works have their springs (*fontana* in Italian can mean simply "spring"). The Dantean interest of Williams was more direct than that of Tolkien: he published his study of Dante's poetry, *The Figure of Beatrice,* in 1943. Some critics have seen Dantean echoes in Williams's second book of Arthurian poetry, *The Region of Summer Stars,* and in his final novel, *All Hallows' Eve*; but no Dantean parallels from them will be argued here.

In short, the Inklings were concerned with *The Divine Comedy* during the war years. This is not to say that Dante explains all of the likenesses in these works. Both Tolkien and Lewis used images of far mountains as a symbol of Heaven; both have their main characters met by a shepherdlike guide. Painters discussing the painting of light appear in *The Great Divorce* and *All Hallows' Eve* (chap. 2)—a similarity that is especially striking since both works were read aloud to the Inklings as they were composed and both appeared in 1945. But Dante gets the emphasis because *The Great Divorce* is an imitation of *La Divina Commedia.*

The above paragraphs may seem an overloading of Lewis's slight book with heavy background. One contrast to Dante that will strike any reader is that Lewis's book is episodic and without Dante's thematic, underlying structures. The narrative line in *The Great Divorce* is simple: Lewis's ghost, in what is revealed at the end of

the book as a wartime dream, is in an urban Hell and there boards
a bus for an excursion to the rural outskirts of Heaven. Lewis makes
clear that these images, and the trip itself, are not to be taken as
doctrine; they are simply a way of setting up a presentation of a
choice a soul has to make between overriding self-love (damnation)
and love of God (salvation)—the "great divorce" of the title. In
this rural landscape Lewis sees a number of encounters between souls
from Hell and either angels or saved souls who have come to meet
them. Most of these meetings end with the ghost from Hell returning there; one ends in the soul being saved; several are not
concluded in Lewis's presence. Lewis himself is met by George
MacDonald, whose *Phantastes* first influenced Lewis's teenage imagination toward the Christian God—although Lewis is more guided
by MacDonald (as Dante by Virgil and Beatrice) than asked to make
a choice.

There seems to be no pattern to the episodes of choice: the Big
Ghost, who wants his rights, is met by Len, his earthly employee
and a murderer; the ghost of an apostate bishop is met by Dick,
his earthly friend; Ikey, who is trying to carry off a golden apple,
is spoken to by an angel; the Hard-Bitten Ghost, not met by anyone,
announces that Heaven is just a propaganda device, that no one
could actually stay there; an overly modest, shamefilled female Ghost
is met by a naked male Spirit; and so forth. This list only takes the
book up to Lewis's meeting with MacDonald, but it is indicative:
Pride, Apostasy, Covetousness, Cynicism, Shamefulness—but no
pattern. [14]

Lewis later puts two examples of human loves that have become
tyrannical side by side; they illustrate some of his comments in *The
Four Loves* (published fifteen years later), but no comparison between
them is made in *The Great Divorce*. The first involves a wife who
has driven her husband, Robert, into a path of worldly success in
their human lives and now wants him back under her control in
the afterlife; she is met by Hilda, perhaps Robert's sister. The second
involves Pam, who wants her son, Michael, back, to live with him—
and, in her understanding, for him—always; she is met by her
brother Reginald. As elsewhere, the type sketches—the dramatic
presentations of Characters, to use a seventeenth-century term—are
vivid; but the structural principle is unclear.

Two other aspects reinforce a reader's feeling of lack of organization. First, the book seems to have been set from its original

(religious) newspaper publication because it follows some of the unlikely breaks in the material that appeared there (e.g., in the middle of Sarah Smith's meeting with her husband, Frank). (Lewis's manuscript does not seem to be extant; the American edition adds chapter numbers to those breaks in the British edition that occurred at the top of pages—which simply confuses matters more.) Second, Lewis shifted his mode of presentation of the souls from Hell as he got near the end of his volume: they suddenly have symbolic additions. The penultimate Character is the Ghost with a red lizard (lustful thoughts) on his shoulder; he is met by an angel. The ultimate is a small ghost, Frank Smith, who leads his tragedian persona by a chain; as indicated above, he is met by his wife, Sarah. Perhaps for Lewis, with his background of study of medieval allegories, these were climactic examples; but surely, for many readers, they are different in type and give an effect of a break in the book.

But many readers have enjoyed *The Great Divorce,* usually reading it primarily for religious and/or moral reasons. The examples of human sins—and of stubbornness in retaining sins—are vividly brought to life. For example, the Grumbler:

"Oh, my dear, I've had such a dreadful time, I don't know how I ever got here at all, I was coming with Elinor Stone and we'd arranged the whole thing and we were to meet at the corner of Sink Street; I made it perfectly plain because I knew what she was like and if I told her once I told her a hundred times I would *not* meet her outside that dread Marjoribanks woman's house; not after the way she'd treated me."

The topic of the afterlife, although here hedged around with qualifications about its presentation, is one that has fascinated many readers. Lewis's images of the "physical" hardness of Heaven contrasted to the ghosts from Hell, and of Heaven's expanded size compared to that of Hell itself, bring Lewis's (and Christian orthodoxy's) comparative attitude into imagistic clarity. In short, although some readers will not care for the Christian discussions between George MacDonald and Lewis (like those between Christian and various companions in *The Pilgrim's Progress*), much of the writing is lively and sharply etched, much of the imagery well imagined.

Further, although the whole work suffers in its organization, nevertheless the individual episodes are often nicely handled—particularly that of the apostate bishop. It is framed with the word *broad,* indicating he is, in British terminology, a Broad Churchman. He greets the soul who meets him by hoping his views have broadened out and leaves humming, "City of God, how broad and far." In the preface to *Mere Christianity,* Lewis said that his own position was "not especially 'high,' nor especially 'low,' nor especially anything else"; this satiric Character indicates how thoroughly that latter phrase is to be taken.

Some more Dantean parallels may close this discussion. As indicated, Lewis's realms are not very clearly located in Dantean terms. The city at the first could be called Dante's City of Dis, but the *Inferno* does not use urban imagery beyond that of city walls. The bus driver brushes the hellish atmosphere from his face as the angel did who broke open the city gates for Dante and Virgil (canto 9). (Perhaps the only logical inconsistency in *The Great Divorce* is MacDonald's later statement that only Christ could make Himself small enough to enter Hell; if so, how did the bus driver—by analogy to *The Divine Comedy,* an angel—get down there? Maybe, at the anagogical level, both the gate opener and the bus driver stand for Christ.) The rural imagery—fields, woods, a river—is closest to the Garden of Eden on top of Mount Purgatory, although this appears on a plain with mountains in sight; and the souls who come from those far mountains to meet the souls from Hell are like Beatrice who descends to the Garden to greet Dante. The one who is closest to Beatrice is Sarah Smith who unsuccessfully greets her husband. Lewis's "Is it . . . is it?" echoes Beatrice's "We are, we are/Beatrice" (*Purgatorio,* canto 30). Lewis in a letter (quoted by Carpenter, 194n) said that readers were supposed to recognize the similarities between the two meetings.

A direct reference to Dante is in the meeting of Lewis and MacDonald: Lewis compares his reading of *Phantastes* to Dante's first seeing of Beatrice, as recorded in *The New Life.* MacDonald (standing for his works) is a God-bearing image for Lewis the character (as well as for Lewis the man). "The divine Godbearer" is Charles Williams's phrase for Beatrice in *The Image of Beatrice* (218); that is, she was the image through which Dante found God. Sarah Smith is a potential God-bearing image for her husband in this fiction. Likewise, Dorothy L. Sayers, in her notes to her translation of *Purgatory,* suggests that Statius, who accompanied Dante to the top of Mount Purgatory, does not see Beatrice in the Garden of Eden but sees instead his private God-bearing image.[15] Thus, these three friends similarly understand the concept that is the basis for the meetings in *The Great Divorce*; if a Ghost will properly accept the encounter, the Spirit or the Angel can be the means of God's grace. There is no surprise here in terms of the fiction; but Beatrice and MacDonald show that these are allegories of this life in addition.

Chapter Nine
The Romancer (II)
The Chronicles of Narnia (1950–56)

Why, after a decade and a half of prose for adults, did Lewis, in the 1950s, suddenly publish seven children's books and one poem— "Narnian Suite" (latter half, 1952; whole, in *Poems,* 1964)—laid in the magical kingdom of Narnia? Lewis's enjoyment of children's fiction was mentioned in the biographical chapter, but this does seem a sudden shift.

Perhaps the best way to describe the Chronicles, and to answer this question, is with an equine metaphor: Narnia, out of E. Nesbit by Tolkien. Lewis thought of the Chronicles as being similar to E. Nesbit's children's books that he enjoyed as a boy, mentioning in 1948 he had plans to complete a book in her tradition. Lewis probably was thinking of her three fantasy books about the children named Cyril, Robert, Anthea, and Jane—*Five Children and It* (1902), *The Phoenix and the Carpet* (1904), and *The Story of the Amulet* (1906)— for in the third book, by means of the Amulet, the children journey as far back in time as Atlantis and as far forward as a future Utopia à la H. G. Wells. Admittedly, Lewis's children move to another world, like Lewis Carroll's Alice or George MacDonald's Anodos in *Phantastes,* instead of to different ages; but the magical adventures of a group of siblings seem to have been Lewis's starting place. And perhaps his mention of E. Nesbitt came from his unconscious, for Roger Lancelyn Green convinced him that the journey through a wardrobe in *The Lion, the Witch and the Wardrobe* was taken, down to some of the dialogue between Lucy Pevensie and Mr. Tumnus the Faun, from E. Nesbitt's "The Aunt and Amabel," which Lewis must have read on its magazine appearance in 1908 and, at the conscious level, forgotten.

If the starting point was E. Nesbitt, however many other influences come into individual books, then the overall pattern of the Chronicles, taken according to its internal chronology, probably is indebted to Tolkien's works on Middle-earth. This is a controversial assertion, since Tolkien disliked the Narnian books for their soft-ening of mythology: if Lucy had really met a faun—that is, a satyr[1]—the result would have been a rape, not a tea party. But Lewis had listened to much of Tolkien's *Silmarillion* (1977) in 1929–30, had read *The Hobbit* (1937) before its publication, had listened to *The Lord of the Rings* (1954–55) as it was composed, had written two reviews of *The Hobbit,* and would write two of *The Lord of the Rings* as it appeared in the same period as the Narnian books. Admittedly, Lewis and Tolkien shared a general medieval orienta-tion as a result of their professional interest, and shared a Christian faith, despite their denominational differences, which gave them a biblical pattern of Creation to Day of Judgment; but neither of these, in themselves, explains Lewis's impulse to produce a work that, in its overall pattern, is close to Tolkien's. Perhaps Nesbitt provided the impulse to children's fiction, at least to the first volume written, *The Lion, the Witch and the Wardrobe* (1950); and Tolkien, the form the series was to take.

The following survey covers mainly the Narnian material in the books, not emphasizing (yet mentioning) the children. The most obvious parallels to Middle-earth will be drawn.

First in the internal chronology of the books is *The Magician's Nephew* (1955).[2] Narnia begins in darkness, although the children—Polly Plummer and Digory Kirke—and some others who have ar-rived there via magic rings are able to stand on something—Narnian ground, it turns out to be (chaps. 8–9). A voice begins singing; soon the stars come into existence and sing with the original voice. (This echoes Job 38:7, in its account of creation "When the morning stars sang together.") The first voice sings into being the sun, the vegetation, and the animals. With the coming of the sun, the singer is revealed to be a lion. This is Aslan, who is the Narnian equivalent (with some differences) of Jesus. (His creation of Narnia is based on the statement in the Gospel of St. John 1:3, referring to Christ, the Divine Logos, that "All things were made by him; and without him was not any thing made that was made.") The general parallel with Tolkien is that Ilúvatar (God) and the Ainur (angels) at the first of *The Silmarillion* sing into existence the World, as Tolkien calls it in his old-fashioned diction, meaning the universe. Actually, they sing into existence a model of it, from which the Ainur con-struct the suns and planets. This creation to music in both Lewis and Tolkien is an ancient concept, best known in British literature for its appearance at the first of John Dryden's "A Song for St. Cecilia's Day" (1687).[3]

A minor echo of Tolkien in this creation account occurs in the episode in which Digory's uncle, Andrew Ketterley, who is also in Narnia, loses some gold and silver coins from his pocket. By the next morning, in the creatively charged soil of Narnia, they have produced a Golden Tree and a silver tree (chap. 14). In Middle-earth, Laurelin the Golden and Telperion the Silver are the two trees that give off light for the world before the sun's rising.[4] Lewis's version is almost a parody, particularly in the context of Ketterley's fears of the animals and other problems, of Tolkien's mythic concept; but Lewis's world is intended for children, unlike *The Silmarillion*, and its tone is correspondingly lighter.

An interesting aspect of this creation account, unrelated to Tolkien, is in the gift of speech to some of the animals who had been created: Aslan breathes on them and they can then talk (chaps. 9–10; cf. Ford, "Gift of Speech," "Holy Spirit"). Lewis's biblically oriented reader may think of the creation of Adam (Genesis 2:7), but the animals are here already alive. The passage parallels one of Lewis's letters (LCSL, 237) in which he imagines the first men being called out of the anthropoid stock to be humans, as Abraham was called from his family and city to be the ancestor of the Hebrews. The result of Aslan's breath in this case is to give the animals a rational soul, rather in St. Thomas Aquinas's sense. If this is a symbol of God-directed evolution, here the events, as is appropriate for a child's book, are condensed in time. Tolkien is more of a creationist in *The Silmarillion*.

In *The Lion, the Witch and the Wardrobe* (1950), the four Pevensie children—Peter, Susan, Edmond, and Lucy—enter Narnia through a magic wardrobe, finding a later period of Narnian history. The main connection with the first book is that Queen Jadis of Charn, who entered Narnia with the two children at the creation, is now ruling Narnia and is usually called the White Witch. The generation of the plot is the desire to rescue Mr. Tumnus the Faun from Jadis, by whom he is being punished for not having turned Lucy in when she first came to Narnia by herself.

But the major parallel to Tolkien occurs in the latter portion of the book (chaps. 14–15) in which Aslan substitutes himself for Edmund, who has given himself to the White Witch in exchange (at first) for candy; Aslan is executed. The biblical parallels are obvious. Aslan's sadness on the afternoon before his death suggests Christ's prayer that the cup may pass from Him; the binding, shaving, and vilifying of Aslan, the arrest, beating, and mocking of Christ; the cracking of the Stone Table, the tearing of the curtain of the Temple as well as the earthquake at the rolling away of the stone from Christ's tomb (the latter, Matthew 28:2 only); and Aslan's resurrection at sunrise and his appearance to Lucy and Susan at the Stone Table, the angel's appearance to the two Marys who came at sunrise to the empty tomb (Matthew 28:1–8 only). These are not all the parallels either in this account or in what follows: the freeing of the enchanted statues from the White Witch's castle (chap. 16), for example, seems much like a slightly displaced Harrowing of Hell.[5]

But it is the parallel of Aslan's and Christ's deaths and resurrections that has stuck in the craws of many critics. Lin Carter, in a popular work on fantasy fiction, for example, writes of "a blatantly symbolic Crucifixion-and-Resurrection scene" that "is very much out of place in these pages."[6]

Two things may be said to this. First, it is in a general way parallel to Gandalf's death and resurrection in *The Lord of the Rings*. Gandalf falls in a fight with a Balrog in underground caverns— falls literally, being pulled into the depths. He then chases the Balrog up ancient stairs to the mountain top, where they both die in battle. Gandalf's spirit (if his spirit and body can be separated) is, after a while, sent back to conclude his mission; he is now Gandalf the White, not Gandalf the Grey (bk. 3, chap. 5). With the help of "The Istari" in *Unfinished Tales* (1980) and "Valaquenta" in *The Silmarillion,* a reader can find out the Christian background of this. Gandalf and the Balrog are both Maiar—that is, lesser angels; Gandalf has been incarnated to help the peoples of Middle-earth to fight against Sauron, another Maia. Both the Balrog and Sauron are fallen angels, obviously, unlike Gandalf—that is, they are demons. There *are* theological differences between an incarnated good angel and the incarnated Son of God; but both die, in the ficitonal equivalents, and both are resurrected. A critic cannot even say the means of death are greatly dissimilar: Aslan is killed by the White Witch, who is an archetypal figure of evil much as the Balrog is. Both die protecting others: Aslan, Edmond; Gandalf, the Company of the Ring. The main difference is that Aslan is passive, a sacrifice, and Gandalf is active, a fighter. Although a reader may feel that Tolkien has hidden his Christian analogy more deeply than Lewis has—and, in doing so, has been more artistic—the difference may be one of audience. Tolkien is writing for adults (he thought) in *The Lord of the Rings* who probably would be irritated by obvious parallels to Christ (technically, foreshadowings of Christ, since Middle-earth is supposed to be laid in an ancient earthly setting); Lewis is writing for children, who may not find Aslan's similarity to Jesus as obvious as adults do.

Second, critics who object to the death and resurrection of Aslan may be reacting to what they believe is crude propaganda, written with a cynical use of child's story. It is well to remember that Lewis's conversion to Christianity hinged on an argument over pagan myths of dying and resurrected gods. On 19 September 1931, Lewis, H. V. D. Dyson, and Tolkien spent an evening arguing about Christianity: Dyson and Tolkien told Lewis that the account of Jesus' death and resurrection was a myth, like the pagan myths that he responded to emotionally, but one that was also historically true. Whatever one makes of this in terms of argumentation, it suggests that Lewis is not putting in the episode cynically. At the time he wrote this book, he was not planning the others; therefore, possibly in an attempt to say what he thought important, he included an episode that resonated with his own interests, pre-Christian as well as Christian.

The Horse and His Boy (1954) overlaps in Narnian time with the last chapter of *The Lion, the Witch and the Wardrobe*—the period when the four Pevensies, grown to adults in Narnia, are ruling that country. The plot is based on the attempts of a boy, a girl, and two talking horses to escape from Calormen, a country to the south of Narnia; they have various reasons for wanting freedom—the boy is in danger of being sold into slavery by his foster-father, the girl is being forced into an unwanted marriage, the horses are having to pretend to be dumb animals—and their adventures end with their helping to thwart a Calormene invasion of Narnia. The parallel to Tolkien is one based on the history and geography of Europe; as Peter J. Schakel has noted, the Calormenes "are Moors: they are identified by their dress, weapons, and manners as the traditional enemies in medieval romances" (*Reading with the Heart*, 13–14). Likewise, to the south of Gondor and Mordor in Middle-earth lies such places as Harad and Khand. The main fact known about Harad is that it is a home of Oliphaunts (elephants), which suggests an

African basis; the men of Far Harad are black.[7] Lewis is working from medieval romances about the Saracen; Tolkien is probably more geographic, since he does not give details suggesting a Moslem culture in his prehistorical setting—but they are both generally parallel in their European/African imaginations.

Prince Caspian (1951) begins what may be called the three-volume Caspian cycle in the Chronicles. This first book tells of the rebellion by Prince Caspian and some Narnian followers against the usurping rule of King Miraz, many years after the action of the preceding volume; the Pevensie children are called into Narnia by the blowing of a magic trumpet by Prince Caspian's forces in their need. The war is concluded—or it is supposed to be—with the individual combat of Peter and King Miraz. Actually, the individual combat ends in a general battle, and what concludes the war is the Tolkienian parallel, the coming of the walking trees. This, of course, is an ancient folklore motif, and Shakespeare used it, in a rational way, in *Macbeth*. But it is striking that two fantasists who knew each other and one of whom had heard the other read his work as it was written should use it at approximately the same time. Tolkien is more Northern than Lewis: he adopts the Anglo-Saxon word for giants into his Ents. The Ents and Huorns do march—which is the parallel—on Saruman's Tower and win the battle of Hornburg (*The Lord of the Rings,* bk. 3, chaps. 4, 7–9). Lewis, on the other hand, is semiclassical in his approach. Lucy Pevensie, as she and her siblings go in the company of a dwarf to Prince Caspian's aid, speaks one night to some trees, calling them "Dryads and Hamadryads" (chap. 9), and asks them to wake up. They stir but do not wake. The next night Lucy sees the trees dancing in a stately manner, one of them (in a sort of double vision) looking like "a huge man with a shaggy beard and great bushes of hair" (chap. 10)—rather like Tolkien's Fangorn. In this episode, they are called "wood-gods and wood-goddesses." When the woods march, they are only called "birch-girls," "willow-women," "oak-men," and so forth (chap. 11); however, they are accompanied by Bacchus and Silenus, so the classical motif is continued. It is also notable that Lewis's trees simply chase and capture the Telmarines (chap. 14), unlike Tolkien's Huorns who quietly kill the Orcs—or at least make them vanish. Again, the juvenile emphasis rules Lewis's work—mass slaughters are not appropriate.

In *The Voyage of the "Dawn Treader"* (1952), Lucy and Edmund

Pevensie and their cousin Eustace Scrubbs enter Narnia through a picture—in this case, the picture of a ship. They find themselves on shipboard with King Caspian, who has sailed to seek seven nobles sent by the dead King Miraz to the east. The sea-quest that follows is episodic, but by the end of it Caspian has fallen in love with the daughter of a star met on one island. Her father, the star, is presumably something like an Intelligence, as discussed in *The Discarded Image*, or an Oyarsa, as in the Ransom Trilogy; if so, he has here taken the form of a man while awaiting his rejuvenization and return to the skies. The questers also have sailed to the end of the world (Narnia is flat), in sight of Aslan's country beyond the sun's rising point. In this book, as in *The Horse and His Boy*, the main parallel to Tolkien is geographic, although here with the directions reversed. To the far west of Middle-earth, across the Sea of Belegaer, lies the land Aman, where dwells the Valar (a group of angels)—this is before the world is made round, when it is still flat. Between the two is not a series of islands, as in *The Voyage of the "Dawn Treader,"* but one large island, Númenor; there are also a number of small islands just off the coast of Aman. Whichever the direction, both writers imagined divine lands that can be reached by sea-voyages across flat worlds, rather like the Celtic Isle of the Dead to the west of Europe.

In the third of the Caspian trilogy, *The Silver Chair* (1953), Eustace Scrubb and Jill Pole enter Narnia through a door in their school wall—more precisely, they are on the Mountain of Aslan, not in Narnia, and they are blown by Aslan's breath to Narnia, "into the west of the world" (chap. 2), which suggests (but does not actually prove) the same geographic framework as *The Voyage of the "Dawn Treader."* If there is any Tolkienesque parallel here it is to Taniquetil, the highest mountain in Aman, from which Manwë (an angel) looks eastward at Middle-earth. (Lewis's mountain does not have ice or snow on top, as Tolkien's does.)

Jill and Eustace are sent into Narnia to search for Rilian, the son of Caspian, who is being held captive (it turns out) by the Queen of the Underland. They first head north into the land of giants; Tolkien mentions some stone-giants living in mountains in *The Hobbit* (chap. 4), but drops them from his adult books. Then Jill, Eustace, and a Narnian companion descend into the underworld— into large caves with a sea and with Earthmen serving the queen. Lewis calls the Earthmen gnomes (chap. 10); their role at first is that of the traditional dwarfs of folklore (one meaning of *gnome*), not that of the Paracelsian elementals of the earth (another meaning)—but, after the queen is killed and they and Prince Rilian are loosed from their enchantments, they turn out to be more like elementals, dropping down to the depths of the world where salamanders (another elemental) swim in a river of fire (chap. 14). Tolkien's material most like this is the two chapters in *The Fellowship of the Ring* recounting the journey of Gandalf, Frodo, and others through the Mines of Moria: a journey through partial darkness, past many passageways and chambers cut by dwarves earlier, and finally—in reverse of Lewis—a fiery danger from the depths, the Balrog, and a fall into the depths by only two characters, Gandalf and the Balrog, when Gandalf breaks a bridge to stop the Balrog (bk. 2, chaps. 4–5). The Orcs who are in the Mines are slightly like the gnomes who are prepared to fight before they learn that Prince Rilian and his companions are friendly (chap. 13).

The final Narnian book, *The Last Battle* (1956), tells of Narnia's final days and its Last Judgment, just as *The Magician's Nephew* told of its creation. Jill and Eustace return to Narnia—it is revealed only at the end of the story that they were killed on Earth in a train wreck (chap. 16)—to rescue King Tirian who appeared to them on earth in a vision (chap. 4); it is about two hundred years after their rescue of Rilian (chap. 5). The forces opposed to Tirian are several: Shift the Ape has dressed Puzzle the Donkey in a lion's skin and has proclaimed him Aslan returned (the Antichrist motif from Matthew 24:23–24), the Calormenes are in league with Shift, the Calormene god Tash (a demon in Narnian terms) comes north, and a number of dwarfs declare themselves on neither side. Eventually Tirian and his side lose, and Aslan ends Narnia with a number of events that echo the Book of Revelations and other apocalyptic New Testament passages. For example, Aslan sits at the door to the new Narnia (like the New Heavens and New Earth of Revelations 21:1; the archetypal Narnia in Platonic terms) while all the creatures come up to him—some turn aside into darkness, others enter in; this is a version of the parable of the sheep and the goats in Matthew 25:31–46 (chap. 14). Peter Pevensie closes the doors to Narnia and locks them with a golden key (chap. 14) in a reminiscence of St. Peter as the Gatekeeper to Heaven (cf. Matthew 16:19). The last two chapters are spent in a description of the characters' journey further into the new Narnia. This conclusion—the salvation of the

protagonists and their meeting with earlier inhabitants of Narnia—
is equivalent to what Tolkien calls the Eucatastrophe, the good turn
at the end of the fairy tale, in his essay "On Fairy-Stories." Strictly
speaking, Tolkien's Middle-earth has nothing like this—at least,
if Tolkien wrote a version of it, it has not been published. But there
are four references to Middle-earth's Day of Doom in *The Lord of
the Rings* and eight references in *The Silmarillion* (Foster, "End"):
then evil will be defeated in "the Last Battle" (Tolkien uses the
phrase), Middle-earth will be cured of its wounds, and the Second
Music will sound.

Literally, no number of parallels can prove an indebtedness, but
here the use of common motifs is impressive and suggestive of
influence. Further, this survey of parallels between Middle-earth
and Narnia is not meant to indicate that Lewis is a simple copyist.
Tolkien and Lewis shared biblical, medieval, and Nordic cultures;
years of hearing Tolkien's works read had further impressed the
images into Lewis's imagination. But everywhere Lewis transforms
these common images with a new handling. Sometimes his handling
is more obvious, as with the death and resurrection of Aslan; sometimes Lewis is more detailed, as with the Arabian-like culture to
the South; sometimes he seems to be doing a simple reversal, as
with the holy lands and a tall mountain to the east, not west, of
Narnia.[8]

The general parallel between Tolkien and Lewis as creators has
been suggested. Tolkien in "On Fairy-Stories" called for the writer
as a subcreator to make a Secondary World with its own laws. This
is not a completely original position: A. G. Baumgarten in 1735
argued that all literature (not just fairy stories) is made up of het-
erocosmoses;[9] Sir Philip Sidney, in the sixteenth century in *Defence
of Poetry,* said the poet brought forth a golden world, in contrast
to the real world of brass (sec. 3). Tolkien was bothered as an artist
that Lewis's fauns did not obey their own nature, for (Tolkien
thought) they were fixed myths that could be introduced into a
Secondary World only as the myth had been established. It is true
that Tolkien himself elevated the nature of his elves in *The Lord of
the Rings,* but at least their beauty often had been there originally.
Lewis elevated the nature of Mr. Tumnus more radically; also, no
tea parties exist in Grecian legend; that is, he changed the nature
of the myth. Other critics are upset over Aslan's death and resurrection; the Secondary World is not separate enough from the Pri-

mary World. This is also the argument of Roger Lancelyn Green over the appearance of Father Christmas in *The Lion, the Witch and the Wardrobe* (chap. 10): what is a symbol tied to a Christian celebration in the Primary World doing in the Secondary (cf. G&H, 241)? Whatever the flaws in Lewis's Narnia (and these three examples come from the first book written), the overall pattern of a world—a Secondary World—parallel in some details to the Bible and in others to Middle-earth, is apparent.

But these likenesses to Tolkien are not all the probable borrowings. Lewis also echoes Dante in the heptology. For an obvious example, there seem to be a number of Garden of Eden-topped hills in Narnia, where the image comes both from Dante's *Purgatorio* and from Milton's imitation of Dante in *Paradise Lost.* The closest to Dante and Milton is the green hill in the Western Wilds that has an earthen wall around an orchard (*The Magician's Nephew,* chap. 13); the version in new Narnia (*The Last Battle,* chap. 16) has the Narnian equivalent of Adam and Eve on the thrones, and, when Lucy and Mr. Tumnus look down from the garden, it turns out to be on the top of a high, stony mountain. The hill, topped with a garden and a central pool, seen in Eustace Scrubb's dream vision in *The Voyage of the "Dawn Treader"* (chap. 7), seems to be related— both to the other hills here and to the mountain-top valley with a pool at the end of *Perelandra.* Finally, the Mountain of Aslan that appears at the first and end of *The Silver Chair* seems to be another Dantean variation.

Among several other possibilities of Dantean influence, the most interesting suggestion has been made by Marsha A. Daigle: that the voyage of the *Dawn Treader* is suggestive of Dante's journey in the *Purgatorio* and the *Paradiso.* Certainly, the Silver Sea of white, water-lily-like flowers at the end of the voyage, before three of the voyagers meet Aslan at the edge of the world (chap. 16), and Dante's vision of Heaven as white rose (cantos 30–32), before his concluding vision of God (canto 33), suggest the imagistic likeness. [10]

In his essay "Sometimes Fairy Stories May Say Best What's to be Said," Lewis speaks of the attraction of the fairy-tale genre for him when he considered what to make of his mental images at the time he wrote the Narnian books: no emphasis on love or close psychology, brevity, restrained description, generic flexibility, and lack of digressions. With the decision to use the genre came also limits on vocabulary. These items sum up the artistry of the Narnian tales fairly well. Perhaps one should add that Lewis often uses complex, traditional images (the garden-topped hills are an example) that replace the richness that would come in adult works from vocabulary.

Till We Have Faces (1956)

Lewis's final book-length fiction has an origin both like and unlike the earlier works. When Lewis wrote *Till We Have Faces: A Myth Retold,* the Inklings were past history and Roger Lancelyn Green, who read and gave advice on the Narnian manuscripts, was no longer his critic; for the book appeared in the year that Lewis first married Joy Davidman. One of Lewis's stepsons, Douglas Gresham, has described the writing: "I know that the character of Orual . . . was written not only by Jack [Lewis], but also by my mother, . . . and the character does contain elements of both people."[11] Davidman herself described the process (in a letter to her first husband) as editorial work on her part: "I can tell [Lewis] how to write more like himself!"[12] No doubt both statements are true. On the other hand, the basic concept of the retelling of the Psyche and Cupid myth—that Pysche's palace would be invisible to her sister—had been with Lewis since 1922; so the basic concept was his. (In what follows, Lewis's name will be used alone, for it is his name on the by-line; but Davidman is, to some degree, responsible for the book. And it is dedicated to her.)

The "myth retold," as indicated, is the tale that first appeared as an inserted story in Apuleius's Latin novel, *Metamorphoses; or, The Golden Ass.* Lewis sets the episode in an imaginary kingdom of Glome, north of Greece and Macedonia, during late classical times. Many of the details are realistic—slavery, pigkilling, worship of a fertility goddess in the form of a stone—although this is still a Lewisian romance and a god (a pagan god foreshadowing Christ) appears, as well as swordplay and visions. The volume is Lewis's least explicitly Christian book-length fiction; but the reason it is his best fiction is not that—rather, it is because *Till We Have Faces* also contains in Orual his best, most complex, characterization.

Lewis intended his book to be titled *Bareface,* a phrase that reverberates throughout the fiction. The publisher wanted a different title, and Lewis suggested *Till We Have Faces.* The latter choice ties to the major themes of (mainly spiritual but also psychological) maturation, although the one time that this phrase is used (bk. 2, chap. 4) is in a religious context. In short, the title as chosen may be misleading so far as the broad meaningfulness of the book is concerned.

The reason that *Bareface* was the better choice is that this is a fiction about an ugly woman. Lewis wisely never tries to describe Orual's ugliness, but lets people make comments on it as she is growing up (e.g., bk. 1, chap. 1). Orual wears a veil in her adult life in public (bk. 1, chap. 16), realizes late in life that going without the veil is now a disguise for her (bk. 2, chap. 2), and in the climactic vision is stripped bare to make her complaint against the gods (bk. 2, chap. 3). Other veilings and unveilings occur in the book. Ultimately, she learns, the ugliness that is hidden or revealed is as much psychological as physical.

As these comments indirectly indicate, this fiction is a growing-up story, a bildungsroman. Orual tells her own story (she is writing her account near the end of her life, in Greek, on a scroll). It seems likely that Lewis's choice of form was influenced by his experience of writing his autobiography, *Surprised by Joy*, published the year before *Till We Have Faces*. It had taught him, probably, a greater inwardness than the writing of his earlier books had.

Orual begins with the death of her mother (Lewis's mother had died when he was nine), although the point is the slaves comment on the cutting of Redival's golden hair—Redival is Orual's sister—and not on Orual's (bk. 1, chap. 1). The focus from the first is on Orual's ugliness, and others' beauty. When a Greek slave, Lysias "the Fox," is used as a tutor for the princesses, Orual turns in love toward him and his teaching of philosophy and poetry, emotionally abandoning her sister. (Orual does not realize this until later [bk. 2, chap. 1].) Then, when Orual takes over the raising of her half-sister, Istra (in Glomish) or Psyche (in Greek), upon the next queen's death in childbirth, her happiness is complete (bk. 1, chap. 2). Psyche is beautiful, and Orual, again in ways she does not understand until later, possesses beauty in possessing her.

When Psyche is grown—her precise age is not clear but she is taller than Redival (bk. 1, chap. 4)—during a time of drought, she is sacrificed to the god of the Grey Mountain, being tied to a sacred tree on the mountain and abandoned. Psyche's confession to Orual, on what she believes is her last night of life, that she has felt a longing for the Grey Mountain (bk. 1, chap. 7) is like the *Sehnsucht* Lewis felt in Belfast for the Castlereagh Hills: this, the source of the journey to the mountains in *The Pilgrim's Regress* and *The Great Divorce,* and less direct treatments in other books, is an image that had remained with Lewis throughout his life. Later in *Till We Have Faces* it is suggested that the gods flow in and out of humans as the gods flow in and out of each other (bk. 2, chaps. 2–3); however that may be, Lewis as the fictional creator certainly flows in and out of his characters. The Fox, for an example not involving *Sehnsucht,* examines actions for their accordance with nature (e.g., bk. 1, chaps. 1–2); he is, in short, in the same natural-law tradition as the Lewis of *The Abolition of Man.*

The sacrifice of Psyche and Orual's meeting with her, alive, afterwards in the valley beyond the ridge with the tree on it (bk. 1, chap. 9) involve some of Lewis's basic changes in Apuleius's story. The god's house is invisible to Orual (bk. 1, chap. 12), although she catches a momentary glimpse of it after she drinks of the stream in that valley—which she immediately doubts, in the fog (bk. 1, chap. 12). (Unlike Apuleius, the third sister is not involved at all.) Psyche's prohibition against seeing her divine husband is like that in the Latin novel, but Orual's eventual means of forcing her to break her promise and to light a lamp is a vivid threat of suicide (bk. 1, chap. 14)—emotional blackmail of her half-sister and foster daughter. Orual's reason, which she does not understand at the time, is the desire to have Psyche to herself; she only realizes it in the final vision, when her complaint against the gods turns out to be a statement of her hatreds (bk. 2, chap. 3). The insight into human possessiveness is not new in Lewis; several of the ghosts in *The Great Divorce* show it. What *is* new is the nonsatiric method of presentation.

In the years that follow her loss of Psyche, Orual becomes queen of Glome, wears her veil, and tries to repress all thoughts of those earlier times. (Lewis builds a transition from the one period to the other with an episode involving a sword fight [bk. 1, chaps. 17–19]; in Frye's terms, it is a high mimetic episode following a romantic one [33–34]: certainly the tone shifts, but the narrative movement is important at that point to carry the reader through the transition.) These years end when Orual, in age, meets a priest of the new goddess Psyche, whose account of his goddess is a mixture of Apuleius (the palace is visible and the two sisters are jealous of it) and a nature myth (bk. 1, chap. 21). Orual's resolve to publish the true account is the catalyst for her writing. The tone of this first part of the volume, these twenty-one chapters, is set by this event: the gods have lied, have sent a false account into the world, concerning Psyche and Orual. Orual says several nasty things about the gods (e.g., bk. 1, chaps. 8, 9, 20), which makes this very unlike the usual Lewis book. If one needs an autobiographical reading here, this is like the early Lewis, before his conversion, in his antitheistic phase of *Spirits in Bondage;* for Orual, the period lasts longer than it did for Lewis, although there is a time in it when she does not think of the gods (bk. 1, chap. 21).

The reversal, the *peripeteia,* comes in book 2, the last four chapters. Biographically, this corresponds to Lewis's conversion; fictionally, to John in *The Pilgrim's Regress* when he had to turn about and go the opposite direction. (Again, it is not that Lewis says something new in this book: rather, it is how he says what he knows about life.) The form the reversal takes is not autobiographical, however, for Orual receives a series of visions—adapted from the tasks Psyche had to perform, or—in one case—the first suicide she attempted, in Apuleius's story. The final vision begins that way also but modulates into a condensed version of Dante's journey in *The Divine Comedy* (with the fourth task of Psyche reshaped in pictures toward the end of the account, replacing perhaps the allegorical pageants Dante saw on top of Mount Purgatory).

Earlier, after Orual blackmailed Psyche into breaking the ban and looking at her husband, the god appeared to Orual and said, "You also shall be Psyche" (bk. 1, chap. 15). What Orual dreams or envisions is that she does three of the tasks for or along side Psyche, bearing Psyche's burden in them. What Lewis is suggesting at the Christian level is a lesser instance of Jesus bearing the burden of mankind's sins; Charles Williams suggested (and evidently showed) that this could be done among humans, and Lewis later bore his wife's pain for her (cf. Dorsett, 126–29). So the material is based on Williams's influence.

Materialists of course will believe this a delusion, acceptable as fiction only with the traditional "willing suspension of disbelief"— if then. But in this romance, it can be defended as symbolism. Orual had destroyed Psyche's marriage through her own maternal possessiveness; now realizing it, partly at an unconscious level (bk. 2, chap. 2), she does what she can to serve Psyche, to help her with her problems. Literally, in the story, this can be dismissed as a type of emotional projection, costing her nothing (Orual serves in dreams;

Psyche is literally not there). But obviously, since Orual in the story
approaches death as the visions take their toll on her (bk. 2, chap.
4)—that is, they do cost her something—the dreams at least sym-
bolize her desire to serve Psyche, to right their relationship if possible, to freely give herself to the one she had hurt.

Again, Psyche's final service to Orual (put in Apuleius's terms
as the bringing of the small box of beauty from Tartarus, here called
the Deadlands) can be dismissed as a rationalization occurring in
the final dream: Orual projects a desire for her forgiveness by Psyche
(bk. 2, chap. 4). But symbolically this is a major point of the book:
it is only as Orual understands her motives, confesses her hatreds,
that she can serve another without unconsciously twisting her service
by her own selfishness. It is only at this point that she, the ugly
sister, can become beautiful.

The Dantean imagery of the final vision (bk. 2, chaps. 3–4)
probably reinforces the religious aspect of the book rather than the
psychological, which has been stressed here. Orual reads her complaint against the gods before a judge of the dead (not treated in
Dantean terms); she sees the Fox and her father, among others, in
her audience. The Dantean echo is "I had not thought before how
many dead there must be," which occurs to Dante on his entrance
to the Vestibule of Hell, where the Indecisive run (canto 3). After
that, the Fox leads Orual away to a three-walled chamber with the
fourth side open to a grassy courtyard and a pool of water. This
suggests Virgil accompanying (rather than leading) Dante to the
top of Mount Purgatory, particularly when Orual identifies the
"blue, fresh sky" as "mountain sky." After they look at some carv-
ings on the three walls, the Fox leads Orual out into the courtyard—
and he is mentioned no more. Virgil also vanishes when Dante
reaches the top of the mountain, although with greater stress (canto
30). In both cases, the protagonists have met their God-bearing
images (in the Charles Williams paraphrase again)—Dante has met
Beatrice, Orual has met Psyche—before, or perhaps as, their guides
disappear. Their reconciliations with the new persons follow. (Orual
is not dipped in the pool as Dante is in Lethe, however.) Finally,
with Psyche beside her, Orual awaits the coming of the god, Psyche's
husband—in a general way parallel to the end of *The Divine Comedy*
with Dante's symbolic vision of God; in this case, Orual's dream-
vision breaks off before she sees him, but she hears his words.

Obviously, these Dantean parallels suggest that a Christian reading of this book is possible. Lewis sees the love of Psyche (Greek for *soul*) and Cupid the god of love (in Apuleius; here the unnamed god of the Grey Mountain) as parallel to the Christian account of the individual soul and God (for "God is love" according to I John 4:8). Orual's reversal of direction (or conversion) leads her at last to Psyche's level. The Dantean parallels simply add to this basic religious framework.

But none of these Dantean or more general religious suggestions invalidate the psychological study traced above: they simply suggest the wealth of the romance. Most readers probably will find Orual's growing up, growing old, and final reaching of maturity—a self-awareness and a self-giving in love—as the most meaningful level in the fiction. That Lewis found a way to present such a theme is one indication of why this is his greatest book.

Chapter Ten
A Romantic and Argumentative Oeuvre
Anatomies and Romances

The two sides of Lewis's personality that were stressed at the beginning of the biographical sketch were the rationalistic and the romantic. These make a curious, and not-too-likely, combination in a person; but they explain in a general way Lewis's works.

The argumentative side found its way into his early Christian apologetics, with their neat use of dilemmas and other rhetorical devices. The natural-law philosophy of the 1940s is also argumentative. Finally, much of the literary criticism has the same temper, particularly *The Personal Heresy,* which simply *is* a literary debate, and *A Preface to "Paradise Lost,"* which answers a number of Milton's critics. Even late in Lewis's life, *An Experiment in Criticism* is indirectly arguing with F. R. Leavis and his followers. (Perhaps the indirect approach is best, for the Leavis position is long lasting, while the individual who occupies it changes.)

If one associates with rational argument a different form of attack and defense, the use of satire and irony, then to Lewis's argumentative works may be added *The Screwtape Letters* and much of *The Pilgrim's Regress.* Northrop Frye calls the argumentative and satiric fictional form, as has been noted, the "anatomy," including in it both Platonic dialogues and *Gulliver's Travels.* The half-essayic, half-fictional upside-down view of the world in *The Screwtape Letters* seems much like what Frye describes.

The other side of Lewis's personality flowed into much of his fiction. The Ransom Trilogy, the Chronicles of Narnia, *Till We Have Faces* are romances, not novels. His narrative poetry—*Dymer,* "The Nameless Isle, "The Queen of Drum"—fit this category also. These are stories and poems about such things as a woman's flight to faerie, a man's fight with a demon on another planet, two children's quest for a lost prince after receiving advice from a talking lion. Clearly Lewis's imagination was not one tied to realism and this socioeconomic, or political, or slice-of-life, world. And some of Lewis's nonfiction, such as *Surprised by Joy* with its theme of the appeal of *Sehnsucht,* are romantic in a rather Wordsworthian way.

But Lewis's works are often not either/or; rather, they are both/ and. *The Pilgrim's Regress,* in addition to its satiric sketches of the views of the 1920s, has at its core John's search for a mountainous island seen in a vision. *Perelandra* has not only the elaborately described Eden of another world and a Dantean journey at the end, but also a fairly normal debate between Ransom and the Un-man with Tinidril as audience-to-be-convinced. Even in *Till We Have Faces,* Orual finds herself caught between two views of Psyche's fate before she forces Psyche to look at her husband: the Fox believes that Psyche is mad and that a criminal living in the hills has taken advantage of her (reason); Bardia, the captain of the King's Guard, believes she is living with a god but that the god is horrible in appearance (myth). Orual comments: "I was the child of Glome and the pupil of the Fox; I saw that for years my life had been lived in two halves, never fitted together" (bk. 1, chap. 13). This is true also for Lewis. It is no wonder that Frye calls the hybrid of the romance and the anatomy (in words that have been quoted before) a "rare and fitful combination."

Lewis's Popularity and Critical Repute

What is the effect of these two stresses—in both senses of the word—on Lewis's readership and on his reputation? The first of these is not difficult to answer. Lewis is the rare example of a writer almost all of whose sixty-some books are in print twenty years after his death. There is no doubt about his popularity. His literary studies are a special case—no doubt they stay in print partly because of their merits, partly because of Lewis's name, and partly because of the retentive natures of the Oxford and Cambridge University presses. But the other books—fiction and nonfiction—are the surprise, compared to the normal situation of an author's books.

Probably much of Lewis's readership is more interested in Christian themes than in artistry. In the terms of Lewis's *Experiment in Criticism,* more interested in *Logos* than on *Poiema.* But this cannot be a full answer. Many Christian books—many by writers as knowledgeable as Lewis in various areas—have been published, reviewed, read by small or large audiences, and then have vanished from the general view. Whether or not Lewis's readers are aware of it, they are responding, in part, to Lewis's art.

One wonders if they also respond to the combination of the argumentative and the romantic: many Christian writers are ready to give an argument (probably backed up with citations of the Bible or of St. Thomas Aquinas), many commercial writers are producing fantasy trilogies, many vanity-press writers are telling of their mystical experiences (or trips in Flying Saucers). But few combine these traits in at all a disciplined way.

At any rate, the popularity has been earned. This book has suggested that Lewis shaped his artistry for different audiences. *Mere Christianity,* one of his best selling and most popular works, was deliberately simplified for a radio audience, for example. (The *Reader's Digest* demonstrates that, in America, very professional simplifications have a great appeal.) *The Abolition of Man,* on the other hand, was written for a learned audience. A like contrast could be made between the simple diction and characterization of the Chronicles of Narnia, as is appropriate in children's books, and the greater richness and psychological depth of *Till We Have Faces.*

The point is the general one of Lewis's generic and audiencial professionalism. It also puts Lewis at odds with many semiromantic celebrations of art for art's sake, or for coterie's sake, or for the artist's own sake, in the twentieth century. This no doubt has hurt Lewis's reputation ("He's a sort of Christian journalist, not a real writer").

Two other matters have also hurt Lewis's critical repute. First, his Christian themes in this "post-Christian" age. (One thinks of F. R. Leavis, forced into spelling out his humanistic assumptions when confronted with, and rejecting, *The Four Quartets.*) Second, Lewis's writing of optimistic romances in a period when the highest praise has gone to realistic or naturalistic novels. Even when fables or (ironic) romances have been found acceptable, they have been pessimistic: *The Trial, Brave New World, Animal Farm, No Exit* (if a play may be included), *The Lord of the Flies, Waiting for Godot* (another play).

But time will take care of these objections. When the first sixty years of the twentieth century are simply another historical period, the era will be considered one like the late Victorian, filled with a diversity of impulses—the Christian, one impulse out of many.

Already (as has been said) a witty term, "the Anglican Revival," has been invented to refer to figures like T. S. Eliot, W. H. Auden, and Edwin Muir. Surely Dorothy L. Sayers, Charles Williams, Christopher Fry—and Lewis—could be safely categorized with them ("Lewis, one of the interesting writers of the so-called 'Anglican Revival,' . . ."). And, if the present author is correct, Lewis, on the basis of *Till We Have Faces,* ranks with the best of them.

Lewis's Works as Great Literature

What, then, are the lasting works upon which the claim for Lewis's greatness rests? This question really will not be answered until the copyrights expire in 2013. What works then will be reprinted? What works will achieve the status of such series as Everyman's Library and Oxford Standard Authors? What works will have a permanent literary demand?

No doubt *Mere Christianity* and some of the other religious nonfiction will appear in collections of Christian classics, but that is not, ultimately, an appeal to the general reader. No doubt the literary histories and other related works will continue to be quoted (and consulted by graduate students on microfische or the equivalent); but that, again, is not the broad, general appeal that great literature has. The present writer will predict that makers of light-verse anthologies will eventually discover such gems as "The Prodigality of Firdausi." (Already, Kingsley Amis, in *The New Oxford Book of English Light Verse* [1978], has reprinted "Evolutionary Hymn.") But even if these verses are reprinted for centuries, that is only a limited claim to greatness.

Even *The Abolition of Man* seems aside from strict belles lettres, as much as the present writer admires it and wishes (vainly wishes) its arguments for natural law might be considered in a fragmented world.

Finally then, for an estimate, here are five works or series on which the claim for Lewis's greatness may be based. The writer regrets the omission of such books as *A Grief Observed* and *Out of the Silent Planet,* but the following seem to him to have the greatest claim. The Chronicles of Narnia present a limited claim, to importance in the field of children's literature; but several examples of significant writers with some works for children can be found in the twentieth century—Isaac Bashevis Singer, for instance. And *The*

Old Possum's Book of Practical Cats is either light verse or children's verse—perhaps both. *The Silver Chair* and *The Last Battle* seem the best of Lewis's series.

Of the nonfiction, here are listed *Surprised by Joy* and *The Four Loves*—despite some flaws in both—and *The Screwtape Letters*. The autobiography, if nothing else, should claim a minor place in Irish literature for its description of a Belfast childhood. But it also is interesting in its depiction of a father-son conflict, the horrors of some English schooling, and the influence of the type of low-level mysticism that Lewis calls *Sehnsucht*. *The Four Loves* is one of those borderline works, like Emerson's essays, that is both belles lettres and philosophy. It has the merit of being on a universal topic.

Of *The Screwtape Letters* and the final work, *Till We Have Faces,* little can be added to the earlier discussions. The former is a series of moral and religious essays, told with the ironic reversal of authorial point of view. The tradition of moral epistles goes back to Seneca's series to Lucilius, but seldom has an essay series been helped in interest as easily as are these by the device of demonic advice. *Till We Have Faces* also allows Lewis to escape his own voice, as his greatest imaginative creation, Queen Orual, tells her own story. The depiction of a pagan kingdom is well sustained, as myth, psychology, detail, and vision here come together.

Notes and References

Chapter One

1. The two best general biographies at the time of this writing are *C. S. Lewis: A Biography* by Roger Lancelyn Green and Walter Hooper (New York: Harcourt Brace Jovanovich, 1974) and *The Inklings* by Humphrey Carpenter (Boston: Houghton Mifflin, 1979). Biographical facts in this book are based on these. A critical citation of the former book in a later chapter will be by G&H. In general, subsequent citations of a book mentioned in a footnote will be by the author's last name; exceptions are noted in the first footnote reference.

2. *Surprised by Joy* (London: Geoffrey Bles, 1955), chap. 1; hereafter cited in text as SJ. Because most of Lewis's books appear in a number of editions, often with different pagination, they are cited in this book only by chapter (or other division), except for three books of letters. Hereafter, these chapter citations will appear in the text without previous footnote citation. (Most of the scholarly books have indexes that will supplement these chapter references.)

3. Corbin Scott Carnell, *Bright Shadow of Reality* (Grand Rapids: Eerdmans, 1974), 87–91.

4. Lewis's essays can most easily be located through the index that accompanies Walter Hooper's "A Bibliography of the Writings of C. S. Lewis: Revised and Enlarged," in *"C. S. Lewis at the Breakfast Table,"* ed. James T. Como (New York: Macmillan, 1979), 277–88.

5. John Wain, "Great Clerk," in Como, 69.

6. For his defeat of Tillyard, see John Lawlor, "The Tutor and the Scholar," in *Light on C. S. Lewis,* ed. Jocelyn Gibb (London: Geoffrey Bles, 1965), 68; for his defeat by Anscombe, see Derek Brewer, "The Tutor: A Portrait," in Como, 58–59. Not all writers on Lewis admit that he was defeated by Anscombe.

7. Nevill Coghill, "The Approach to English," in Gibb, 57.

8. George Sayer, "Jack on Holiday," in Como, 203.

9. *They Stand Together,* ed. Walter Hooper (London: Collins, 1979), 167, 208. Lewis seems to have first referred to his sexual bias in 1915 without Greeves understanding him (75). Subsequent references are given parenthetically in the text.

10. Owen Barfield, "Introduction," in Gibb, ix–xii.

11. Derek Brewer, in Como, 62.

12. Ibid., 48.

13. Kathleen Raine, "From a Poet," in Gibb, 102–3.

14. Printed in *They Stand Together*, 554; photographed in a readable fashion in Douglas Gilbert and Clyde S. Kilby, *C. S. Lewis: Images of His World* (Grand Rapids: Eerdmans, 1973), 65.

Chapter Two

1. In an 8(?) November 1945 letter to Herbert Edward Palmer, in the Humanities Research Center, University of Texas at Austin.
2. Northrop Frye, *Anatomy of Criticism* (Princeton: Princeton University Press, 1957), 307–8.
3. *Letters of C. S. Lewis*, ed. W. H. Lewis (London: Geoffrey Bles, 1966), 206; hereafter cited in text as LCSL.
4. *Letters to an American Lady*, ed. Clyde S. Kilby (Grand Rapids: Eerdmans, 1967), 70–71; hereafter cited in text as LAL.

Chapter Three

1. This essay appears in *Patterns of Love and Courtesy*, ed. John Lawlor (Evanston: Northwestern University Press, 1966), 26–44.
2. Helen Gardner, "Clive Staples Lewis: 1898–1963," *Proceedings of the British Academy* 51 (n.d. in pamphlet form): 427.
3. Cf. Walter R. Davis (ed.), *The Works of Thomas Campion* (1967; reprint, New York: Norton, 1970), 128.
4. This was pointed out to the author by Dolores A. Espinosa of Alhambra, California, in a letter of 1 July 1983.
5. Citations of *Studies in Words* will be from the expanded edition (Cambridge: Cambridge University Press, 1967).
6. Edmund Spenser, *The Faerie Queene*, ed. A. C. Hamilton (London: Longman, 1977), 496. Five books by Lewis are listed in the bibliography (749–50) but not *Studies in Words*.
7. For the third possibility, cf. Lewis's unpublished letter of 11 November 1946 to Herbert Edward Palmer in the Humanities Research Center, University of Texas at Austin.
8. There is a similar passage in Owen Barfield's *Saving the Appearances* (London: Faber & Faber, 1957), 76–77; but the whole Barfield/Lewis cross influences are too complex for this book.
9. Lewis, in an undated letter of February 1961, says to his correspondent that he knows existentialism only through the three authors here mentioned in parentheses (LSCL, 297).

Chapter Four

1. Noted by Christopher Derrick, *C. S. Lewis and the Church of Rome* (San Francisco: Ignatius Press, 1981), 193n.
2. For a discussion of Lewis's views of the Bower of Bliss and the

Garden of Adonis, see Margaret Patterson Hannay, "Rehabilitations: C. S. Lewis' Contributions to the Understanding of Spenser and Milton" (Ph.D. diss., State University of New York at Albany, 1976), 116–33.

Chapter Six

1. Peter J. Schakel, *Reason and Imagination in C. S. Lewis* (Grand Rapids: Eerdmans, 1984), 148–49, 199–200.

Chapter Seven

1. Dabney Adams Hart, *Through the Open Door* (University, Ala.: University of Alabama Press, 1984), 108–11.

Chapter Eight

1. Kathleen Raine, *Defending Ancient Springs* (London: Oxford University Press, 1967), 1.
2. Mark R. Hillegas, *The Future as Nightmare* (New York: Oxford University Press, 1967), 133–44. Some ideas in this chapter will be mentioned in the later discussion of *That Hideous Strength*.
3. For fuller details, see Henry Noel, untitled notes, *Bulletin of the New York C. S. Lewis Society* 2, no. 1 (November 1970):6–7. (This was before the publication received its main title of *CSL*.)
4. Angele Botros Samaan, "C. S. Lewis, the Utopist, and His Critics," *Cairo Studies in English,* 1963–66, 137–38.
5. Dabney Adams Hart, "C. S. Lewis's Defense of Poesie" (Ph.D. diss., University of Wisconsin, 1959), 218.
6. Victor M. Hamm, "Mr. Lewis in Perelandra," *Thought* 20 (June 1945):271.
7. See, for example, Hamm, 278–83, and Hannay, "The Interplanetary Novel as Milton Criticism," in "Rehabilitations," 299–342.
8. Tinidril's name is first given in chap. 17 of *Perelandra* (London: John Lane, Bodley Head, 1943); but it is a convenience to use it throughout this discussion.
9. Clyde S. Kilby, *The Christian World of C. S. Lewis* (Grand Rapids: Eerdmans, 1964), 97.
10. Frank Davis Adams, "The Literary Tradition of the Scientific Romance" (Ph.D. diss., University of New Mexico, 1951), 321.
11. Charles Williams, *The Figure of Beatrice* (London: Faber & Faber, 1943), 47 ("Beatrician experience"), 48 ("Beatrician revelation"), 95 ("Beatrician discovery").
12. Humphrey Carpenter, *Tolkien* (Boston: Houghton Mifflin, 1977), 196. References to Carpenter in the text will still refer to *The Inklings*.
13. J. R. R. Tolkien, Foreword to *The Fellowship of the Ring* (New

York: Ballantine Books, 1965), xi. This statement is not in the original hardback edition.

14. Evan K. Gibson, in *C. S. Lewis: Spinner of Tales* (Washington, D.C.: Christian University Press, 1980), argues that there are five ghosts before MacDonald and five after: the first five are inwardly corrupt, the second five work outwardly (116). The numbers are right, but is the young man with the lizard (lust) really outwardly corrupt? Nothing indicates he is a seducer or a womanizer; the lizard whispering in his ear suggests lustful *thoughts*.

15. Dante, *The Divine Comedy: II: Purgatory*, trans. Dorothy L. Sayers (Harmondsworth, Middlesex: Penguin Classics, 1955), 327–28.

Chapter Nine

1. Lewis lists both fauns and satyrs in *The Silver Chair* (London: Geoffrey Bles, 1953), chap. 3; Paul F. Ford, *Companion to Narnia* (San Francisco: Harper & Row, 1980; rev. ed., 1983), in his note under *satyr* says satyrs are more goatlike and sexual than fauns; perhaps so, but most reference books seem to believe them identical. One later reference to Ford's book in the text will be by section listing, so either edition can be consulted.

2. This discussion does not mean the Narnian books should be read in the order of their internal chronology; Peter J. Schakel, *Reading with the Heart* (Grand Rapids: Eerdmans, 1979), 143–45, n. 6, makes a good case for reading them in the order of their publication; so does Ford, near the end of his introduction to both editions of his book.

3. Cf. John Hollander, *The Untuning of the Sky* (1961; New York: Norton, 1970), 240–41 (Cowley's account of creation to music in bk. 1 of *Davideis*), etc.

4. J. R. R. Tolkien, *The Silmarillion* (Boston: Houghton Mifflin, 1977), "Quenta Silmarillion," chap. 1.

5. Hart, "C. S. Lewis's Defense of Poesie," 297.

6. Lin Carter, *Imaginary Worlds* (New York: Ballantine Books, 1973), 106.

7. The blackness is not noted in Robert Foster, *The Complete Guide to Middle-earth* (New York: Ballantine Books, 1978), "Far Harad."

8. For a longer and, at a number of points, different comparison of Narnia and Middle-earth, see this author's "The World of Narnia," *Niekas*, no. 32 (Winter 1983):46–57. A number of similar comparisons have been published.

9. A. G. Baumgarten, *Meditationes philosophicae de nonnullis ad poema pertinentibus* (1733), cited in Graham Hough, *An Essay on Criticism* (New York: Norton, 1966), 12, 17, 77, 130.

10. Marsha A. Daigle, "Dante's *Divine Comedy* and the Fiction of

C. S. Lewis" (Ph. D. diss., University of Michigan, 1984), 200–13. Daigle's dissertation was finished too late for it to be consulted generally for this book; the author thanks Dr. Daigle for sending him a copy of the chapter on the Chronicles of Narnia. (Her dissertation covers almost all of Lewis's fiction, including *The Pilgrim's Regress* and *The Screwtape Letters,* but excluding *Till We Have Faces.*)

11. Doug Gresham, untitled speech, *Ring Bearer* 2, no. 3 (Spring [September] 1984):39.

12. Quoted in Lyle W. Dorsett, *And God Came In* (New York: Macmillan, 1983), 117.

Selected Bibliography

PRIMARY SOURCES

Through 1979 this checklist cites the first editions, as listed in Hooper's bibliography (which is itself listed in the first section of secondary materials); after that date, it lists the editions seen by this author. Editions other than the first complete edition are listed only if they are mentioned in this book. In the cases of *Arthurian Torso, Broadcast Talks, Mere Christianity,* and *A Preface to "Paradise Lost,"* elaborate subtitles have been omitted. Essays by Lewis can be located by Hooper's index.

1. Fiction
Boxen: The Imaginary World of the Young C. S. Lewis. Edited by Walter Hooper. San Diego: Harcourt Brace Jovanovich, 1985. [Juvenilia.]
"The Dark Tower" and Other Stories. Edited by Walter Hooper. London: Collins, 1977.
The Great Divorce: A Dream. London: Geoffrey Bles, Centenary Press, 1945 (dated 1946).
The Horse and His Boy. London: Geoffrey Bles, 1954.
The Last Battle: A Story for Children. London: Bodley Head, 1956.
The Lion, the Witch and the Wardrobe: A Story for Children. London: Geoffrey Bles, 1950.
The Magician's Nephew. London: Bodley Head, 1955.
Out of the Silent Planet. London: John Lane, Bodley Head, 1938.
Perelandra: A Novel. London: John Lane, Bodley Head, 1943.
The Pilgrim's Regress: An Allegorical Apology for Christianity, Reason and Romanticism. London: J. M. Dent, 1933. With author's preface and notes, London: Geoffrey Bles, 1943.
Prince Caspian: The Return to Narnia. London: Geoffrey Bles, 1951.
The Silver Chair. London: Geoffrey Bles, 1953.
That Hideous Strength: A Modern Fairy-Tale for Grown-Ups. London: John Lane, Bodley Head, 1945.
Till We Have Faces: A Myth Retold. London: Geoffrey Bles, 1956.
The Voyage of the "Dawn Treader." London: Geoffrey Bles, 1952.

2. Book-Length Nonfiction
The Abolition of Man; or, Reflections on Education with Special Reference to the Teaching of English in the Upper Forms of Schools. London: Oxford University Press, 1944 (dated 1943).

The Allegory of Love: A Study in Medieval Tradition. Oxford: Clarendon Press, 1936: Rev. 1938.

Beyond Personality: The Christian Idea of God. London: Geoffrey Bles, Centenary Press, 1944.

Broadcast Talks. London: Geoffrey Bles, Centenary Press, 1942. American title: *The Case for Christianity*.

Christian Behaviour: A Further Series of Broadcast Talks. London: Geoffrey Bles, Centenary Press, 1943.

The Discarded Image: An Introduction to Medieval and Renaissance Literature. Cambridge: Cambridge University Press, 1964.

English Literature in the Sixteenth Century, Excluding Drama. Oxford: Clarendon Press, 1954.

An Experiment in Criticism. Cambridge: Cambridge University Press, 1961.

The Four Loves. London: Geoffrey Bles, 1960.

A Grief Observed. London: Faber & Faber, 1961. Originally published as by N. W. Clerk.

Letters to Malcolm: Chiefly on Prayer. London: Geoffrey Bles, 1964.

Mere Christianity. London: Geoffrey Bles, 1952. Contains *Broadcast Talks, Christian Behaviour,* and *Beyond Personality*.

Miracles: A Preliminary Study. London: Geoffrey Bles, Centenary Press, 1947. Chap. 3 rev. London: Collins, Fontana Books, 1960.

A Preface to "Paradise Lost." London: Oxford University Press, 1942.

The Problem of Pain. London: Centenary Press, 1940.

Reflections on the Psalms. London: Geoffrey Bles, 1958.

The Screwtape Letters. London: Geoffrey Bles, 1942. Expanded as *"The Screwtape Letters" and "Screwtape Proposes a Toast."* London: Geoffrey Bles, 1961.

Spenser's Images of Life. Edited by Alastair Fowler. Cambridge: Cambridge University Press, 1967.

Studies in Words. Cambridge: Cambridge University Press, 1960. Exp. 1967.

Surprised by Joy: The Shape of My Early Life. London: Geoffrey Bles, 1955.

3. Books of Essays

Christian Reflections. Edited by Walter Hooper. London: Geoffrey Bles, 1967. Contains 14 essays.

"Fern-Seed and Elephants" and Other Essays on Christianity. Edited by Walter Hooper. London: Collins, Fontana Books, 1975. Contains 8 essays.

"God in the Dock": Essays on Theology and Ethics. Edited by Walter Hooper. Grand Rapids: Eerdmans, 1970. British title: *Undeceptions: Essays on Theology and Ethics*. Contains 48 essays and 12 letters. Note: one of the two paperbacks containing selections from this volume has the main title *"The Grand Miracle,"* which may be confusing.

Of Other Worlds: Essays and Stories. Edited by Walter Hooper. London:

Geoffrey Bles, 1966. Contains 9 essays, 3 stories, and 1 fragment of
a novel; contents later split into *"The Dark Tower" and Other Stories*
and *"On Stories" and Other Essays on Literature*.
"On Stories" and Other Essays on Literature. Edited by Walter Hooper. New
York: Harcourt Brace Jovanovich, 1982. British title: *Of This and
Other Worlds*. Contains 20 essays.
Rehabilitations and Other Essays. London: Oxford University Press, 1939.
Contains 9 essays.
"Screwtape Proposes a Toast" and Other Pieces. London: Collins, Fontana
Books, 1965. Contains 8 essays.
Selected Literary Essays. Edited by Walter Hooper. Cambridge: Cambridge
University Press, 1969. Contains 22 essays.
Studies in Medieval and Renaissance Literature. Edited by Walter Hooper.
Cambridge: Cambridge University Press, 1966. Contains 14 essays.
They Asked for a Paper: Papers and Addresses. London: Geoffrey Bles, 1962.
Contains 12 essays.
"Transposition" and Other Addresses. London: Geoffrey Bles, 1949. American
title: *"The Weight of Glory" and Other Addresses*. Contains 5 essays.
Expanded ed. *"The Weight of Glory" and Other Addresses*. Edited by
Walter Hooper. New York: Macmillan, 1980. Contains 9 essays.
"The World's Last Night" and Other Essays. New York: Harcourt, Brace,
1960. Contains 7 essays.

4. Poetry and Verse
Dymer. London: J. M. Dent, 1926. Originally published as by Clive
Hamilton.
Narrative Poems. Edited by Walter Hooper. London: Geoffrey Bles, 1969.
Contains 3 narrative poems and 1 fragment.
Poems. Edited by Walter Hooper. London: Geoffrey Bles, 1964. Contains
123 poems.
Spirits in Bondage: A Cycle of Lyrics. London: William Heinemann, 1919.
Originally published as by Clive Hamilton. Contains 40 poems.

5. Letters
Letters of C. S. Lewis. Edited by W. H. Lewis. London: Geoffrey Bles,
1966.
Letters to an American Lady. Edited by Clyde S. Kilby. Grand Rapids:
Eerdmans, 1967.
Letters to Children. Edited by Lyle W. Dorsett and Marjorie Lamp Mead.
New York: Macmillan, 1985.
Mark vs. Tristram: Correspondence between C. S. Lewis and Owen Barfield.
Edited by Walter Hooper. Cambridge, Mass.: Lowell House Printers,
1967. Pamphlet of 126 copies.

They Stand Together: The Letters of C. S. Lewis to Arthur Greeves (1914–1963). Edited by Walter Hooper. London: Collins, 1979.

6. Miscellaneous

Arthurian Torso. London: Oxford University Press, 1948. Contains "The Figure of Arthur" by Charles Williams and "Williams and the Arthuriad" by Lewis.

Essays Presented to Charles Williams. London: Oxford University Press, 1947. A festschrift anonymously edited by Lewis.

George MacDonald: An Anthology. Edited by C. S. Lewis. London: Geoffrey Bles, 1946.

The Personal Heresy: A Controversy. London: Oxford University Press, 1939. Contains alternate chapters by Lewis and E. M. W. Tillyard.

The Revised Psalter: Pointed for Use with Anglican Chants. London: Cambridge University Press (and three other publishers), 1966. The revisers were F. D. Coggan, G. A. Chase, J. Dykes Bower, T. S. Eliot, Gerald Knight, Lewis, and D. Winton Thomas.

7. Excerpts

The Business of Heaven: Daily Readings from C. S. Lewis. Edited by Walter Hooper. San Diego: Harcourt Brace Jovanovich, 1984.

The Joyful Christian: 127 Readings from C. S. Lewis. Edited by Henry William Griffin. New York: Macmillan, 1977.

A Mind Awake: An Anthology of C. S. Lewis. Edited by Clyde S. Kilby. London: Geoffrey Bles, 1968.

The Visionary Christian: 131 Readings from C. S. Lewis. Edited by Chad Walsh. New York: Macmillan, 1981.

SECONDARY SOURCES

With a few exceptions in the first following section and two in the second, the secondary checklist is limited to full-length books on Lewis alone; both *CSL* and *Mythlore* contain listings of shorter items. Other periodicals substantially on Lewis are *Canadian C. S. Lewis Journal*, the *Chronicles of the Portland C. S. Lewis Society*, the *Lamp-post of the Southern California C. S. Lewis Society*, the *Ring Bearer*, and *Seven: An Anglo-American Literary Review;* most of them review new books on Lewis or partially on Lewis. In addition, much help is available from the Wade Collection, Wheaton College, Wheaton, Illinois.

1. Bibliographies and Indexes

Bratman, David S. "Subject Index to *Mythlore*, Issues 1–30." *Mythlore* 9, nos. 1/31 (Spring 1982):42–47.

————. "Subject Index to *Mythlore*, Issues 31–39." *Mythlore* 11, nos. 2/
40 (Autumn 1984):61–63. About one-fourth of *Mythlore* is on Lewis.
"CSL: The Bulletin of the New York C. S. Lewis Society": Summary of Contents
of the First One Hundred Issues, 6 pp.; Summary of Contents: Number 101
to Number 131, 2 pp.; Summary of Contents: Number 132 to Number
158, 2 pp. Title indicative; no cross indexing.
Christopher, Joe R. "An Inklings Bibliography," Nos. 1–28. *Mythlore* 3,
no. 4 (June 1976)–11, no. 1 (Summer 1984). Covers Lewis among
others; hit or miss in what it lists; annotated.
————, and Ostling, Joan K. *C. S. Lewis: An Annotated Checklist of Items
about Him and His Works.* Kent, Ohio: Kent State University Press,
n.d. (1974). The basic secondary bibliography through June 1972.
"The Chronicle of The Portland C. S. Lewis Society": Index: February 1972
through December 1984. Six pages with various listings.
Hooper, Walter. "A Bibliography of the Writings of C. S. Lewis: Revised
and Enlarged." In *"C. S. Lewis at the Breakfast Table" and Other
Reminiscences,* edited by James T. Como, pp. 245–88. New York:
Macmillan Publishing Co., 1979. The basic bibliography of Lewis's
published writings, in eight sections; index.
Thorson, Stephen, and Daniel, Jerry. "Bibliographic Notes: Published
Drawings by C. S. Lewis." *CSL* 14, no. 8 (June 1983):6–7. Eleven
listings, although several contain more than one drawing.
————. "Bibliographic Notes: Published Holographs." *CSL* 14, no. 10
(August 1983):6–7. Twenty-six listings.

2. Biographies and Biographical Materials

Arnott, Anne. *The Secret Country of C. S. Lewis.* Grand Rapids: Eerdmans,
1975. For teenagers; not scholarly.
Carpenter, Humphrey. *The Inklings: C. S. Lewis, J. R. R. Tolkien, Charles
Williams, and Their Friends.* Boston: Houghton Mifflin, 1979. A
nonsentimental appraisal of Lewis; a good balance to Green and Hooper.
Como, James T., ed. *"C. S. Lewis at the Breakfast Table" and Other Rem-
iniscences.* New York: Macmillan, 1979. Twenty-four essays, mainly
biographical.
Dorsett, Lyle W. *And God Came In.* New York: Macmillan, 1983. A
biography of Lewis's wife, (Helen) Joy Davidman (Gresham), Amer-
ican, Jewish by background, one-time communist, divorcée.
Gibb, Jocelyn, ed. *Light on C. S. Lewis.* London: Geoffrey Bles, 1965.
Seven essays, largely biographical.
Gilbert, Douglas, and Kilby, Clyde. *C. S. Lewis: Images of His World.*
Grand Rapids: Eerdmans, 1973, A pictorial book, with photographs
(many in color) by Gilbert.
Green, Roger Lancelyn, and Hooper, Walter. *C. S. Lewis: A Biography.*
New York: Harcourt Brace Jovanovich, 1974. The authorized bi-

ography, with a valuable account by Green of the writing of the Narnian books.

Hooper, Walter. *Through Joy and Beyond: A Pictorial Biography of C. S. Lewis.* New York: Macmillan, 1982. A biography with black-and-white photographs; contains brief reminiscences by Owen Barfield and others.

Keefe, Carolyn, ed. *C. S. Lewis: Speaker and Teacher.* Grand Rapids: Zondervan, 1971. Seven essays, four biographical.

Lewis, W. H. *Brothers and Friends: The Diaries of Major Warren Hamilton Lewis.* Edited by Clyde S. Kilby and Marjorie Lamp Mead. San Francisco: Harper & Row, 1982. Large, pleasant selections from the diary of Lewis's brother.

Lindskoog, Kathryn. "Some Problems in C. S. Lewis Scholarship." *Christianity and Literature* 27, no. 4 (Summer 1978):43–61. Raises serious questions about Walter Hooper's veracity over his relationship to Lewis; scholars should consult this before using any personal anecdotes from Hooper's prefaces or books.

Schofield, Stephen, ed. *In Search of C. S. Lewis.* South Plainfield, N.J.: Bridge Publishing, 1983. Contains 25 essays or interviews, and letters, from *Canadian C. S. Lewis Journal;* almost entirely biographical in orientation.

3. General Surveys

Hannay, Margaret Patterson. *C. S. Lewis.* New York: Frederick Unger, 1981. Extensive summaries; good, brief criticism; bibliography.

Kilby, Clyde S. *The Christian World of C. S. Lewis.* Grand Rapids: Eerdmans, 1964. Summaries, with very occasional inaccuracies, of creative and Christian works; mainly thematic and appreciative comments.

Lindskoog, Kathryn. *C. S. Lewis: Mere Christian.* 3d ed. Downers Grove, Ill.: InterVarsity Press, 1981. A survey of Lewis's positions on fifteen topics, including "God," "Nature," "Truth," "Education." A good, popular work; the appendixes include information on such things as Narnian maps.

Walsh, Chad. *C. S. Lewis: Apostle to the Skeptics.* New York: Macmillan, 1949. The first book on Lewis; pleasant but limited by its date.

————. *The Literary Legacy of C. S. Lewis.* New York: Harcourt Brace Jovanovich, 1979. A good, critical survey of Lewis's books, longer in its discussion of the creative works than the critical or Christian; bibliography.

4. Literary Criticism and Aids

Ford, Paul F. *Companion to Narnia.* San Francisco: Harper & Row, 1980. Rev. 1983. An excellent alphabetically arranged handbook of characters, places, motifs, Christian themes, etc.; cross-referenced; notes at the end of the listings often give biographical explanations.

Gibson, Evan K. *C. S. Lewis: Spinner of Tales: A Guide to His Fiction.* Washington, D.C.: Christian University Press, 1980. Includes *The Screwtape Letters,* excludes *The Pilgrim's Regress.* An excellent beginning place: organization, characterization, Christian meanings.

Glover, Donald E. *C. S. Lewis: The Art of Enchantment.* Athens: Ohio University Press, 1981. Establishes Lewis's theory of fiction from his letters and *An Experiment in Criticism,* and applies it to his fiction, tracing developments in artistry and discussing the relationships of forms and meaning.

Green, Roger Lancelyn. *C. S. Lewis.* London: Bodley Head, 1963. A small book on Lewis as a writer for children, discussing *Out of the Silent Planet, Perelandra,* and the Narnian stories.

Hooper, Walter. *Past Watchful Dragons: The Narnian Chronicles of C. S. Lewis.* New York: Collier Books, 1979. A good discussion, perhaps of particular interest for all the early drafts of Narnian materials in chap. 5.

Howard, Thomas. *The Achievement of C. S. Lewis: A Reading of His Fiction.* Wheaton, Ill.: Harold Shaw, 1980. A lively discussion of the themes of the Narnian stories, the Ransom Trilogy, and *Till We Have Faces* (in that order).

Karkainan, Paul A. *Narnia Explored.* Old Tappan, N.J.: Revell, 1979. A Christian explication, sometimes more Christian than Narnian.

Kilby, Clyde S. *Images of Salvation in the Fiction of C. S. Lewis.* Wheaton, Ill.: Harold Shaw, 1978. Extensive summaries (with two errors in that of *Till We Have Faces*); numbered thematic comments and other aids after each retelling.

Lindskoog, Kathryn. *The Lion of Judah in Never-Never Land: The Theology of C. S. Lewis Expressed in His Fantasies for Children.* Grand Rapids: Eerdmans, 1973. A religious study, with comparisons to Lewis's other writings; Lewis praised the first version of this work.

Murphy, Brian. *C. S. Lewis.* Mercer Island, Wash.: Starmount House, 1983. A discussion for a science-fiction readership, emphasizing the Ransom Trilogy but also dealing with the Narnian stories and *Till We Have Faces.*

Sammons, Martha C. *A Guide through C. S. Lewis' Space Trilogy.* Westchester, Ill.: Cornerstone Books, 1980. A good guide to the background materials of the Ransom Trilogy: medieval, Arthurian, biblical, etc.; contains a useful glossary of people, places, Old Solar words.

————. *A Guide through Narnia.* Wheaton, Ill.: Harold Shaw, 1979. On the Narnian materials proper, rather than background as with the book above; contains a Narnian glossary. Largely outdated by Ford (above).

Schakel, Peter J. *Reading with the Heart: The Way into Narnia.* Grand Rapids: Eerdmans, 1979. The best literary criticism of the Narnian stories, which treats them as literature embodying theme.

―――. *Reason and Imagination in C. S. Lewis: A Study of "Till We Have Faces."* Grand Rapids: Eerdmans, 1984. The first half of the book is the best study of *Till We Have Faces* available; the second half discusses Lewis's life and writings in terms of the split between reason and imagination found in Orual.

―――, ed. *The Longing for a Form: Essays on the Fiction of C. S. Lewis.* Kent, Ohio: Kent State University Press, 1977. Fourteen essays; literary criticism on Lewis can be said to start here.

5. Other Studies

Adey, Lionel. *C. S. Lewis's "Great War" with Owen Barfield.* English Literary Studies Monograph Series, no. 14. British Columbia: University of Victoria, 1978. Discusses the 1923/24-through-1930 arguments between the pre-Christian Lewis and Barfield over the latter's anthroposophy and related positions; based largely on unpublished materials here partly quoted.

Aeschliman, Michael D. *The Restitution of Man: C. S. Lewis and the Case against Scientism.* Grand Rapids: Eerdmans, 1983. A good book, although more background to the several-centuries' debate between scientism and values than on Lewis proper.

Beversluis, John. *C. S. Lewis and the Search for Rational Religion.* Grand Rapids: Eerdmans, 1985. A fascinating book that disproves—or makes a good attempt to disprove—all of Lewis's arguments for the existence of God, with some related positions; it appeared too late to be used in this book.

Carnell, Corbin Scott. *Bright Shadow of Reality: C. S. Lewis and the Feeling Intellect.* Grand Rapids: Eerdmans, 1974. The basic study of Lewis's *Sehnsucht.*

Christensen, Michael J. *C. S. Lewis on Scripture: His Thoughts on the Nature of Biblical Inspiration, the Role of Revelation and the Question of Inerrancy.* Waco, Tex.: Word Books, 1979. A moderately successful book on its topic.

Cunningham, Richard B. *C. S. Lewis: Defender of the Faith.* Philadelphia: Westminster Press, 1967. Surveys Lewis's theology and apologetic means, including his fiction; tends to see all as apologetics.

Derrick, Christopher. *C. S. Lewis and the Church of Rome: A Study in Proto-Ecumenism.* San Francisco: Ignatius Press, 1981. An interesting study by a Roman Catholic of why Lewis did not become a Roman Catholic, partly biographical, partly theological.

Hart, Dabney Adams. *Through the Open Door: A New Look at C. S. Lewis.* University: University of Alabama Press, 1984. Not a clearly organized work; the two chapters on Lewis as a teacher (chaps. 5–6) are the best.

Holmer, Paul L. *C. S. Lewis: The Shape of His Faith and Thought.* New York: Harper & Row, 1976. A poor book, jargonish, out of focus; finds subtleties of a type not in Lewis.

Meilaender, Gilbert. *Taste for the Other: The Social and Ethical Thought of C. S. Lewis.* Grand Rapids: Eerdmans, 1978. An excellent discussion of the subtitular matter, which also has much to say about Lewis's theology and the themes of his fiction.

Payne, Leanne. *Real Presence: The Holy Spirit in the Works of C. S. Lewis.* Westchester, Ill.: Cornerstone Books, 1979. Uses passages from Lewis, occasionally arguing beyond them, to present a sacramental, charismatic Christianity, and (in the later chapters) psychological, creative health.

Purtill, Richard L. *C. S. Lewis's Case for the Christian Faith.* San Francisco: Harper & Row, 1981. Sometimes Lewis's arguments nicely analyzed; sometimes Purtill's case for Christianity instead.

Smith, Robert Houston. *Patches of Godlight: The Pattern of Thought in C. S. Lewis.* Athens: University of Georgia Press, 1981. A description of Lewis's world view that underlines his Christianity; a good discussion of Plato; also chapters on the medieval model of the universe, mysticism, and related matters.

White, William Luther. *The Image of Man in C. S. Lewis.* Nashville: Abingdon Press, 1969. Studies Lewis's doctrine of man—Creation, Fall, Redemption, Immortality—both in Lewis's exposition and his fiction; finds him a sophisticated remythologizer.

Willis, John Randolph. *Pleasures Forevermore: The Theology of C. S. Lewis.* Chicago: Loyola University Press, 1983. Such chapters as "Jesus Christ and Redemption," "The Church and Sacraments"; occasional disagreements from a Roman Catholic perspective; mainly summaries and illustrations from the fiction.

Index